WEALTHI

The Average Joe's Guide to Becoming Rich

By Darren Smith

Acknowledgements: A special thanks to Peggy Andersen, Delise Cubie, Kelly Schrader and Barry Smith for helping to edit and make this book possible. I would also be remiss not to thank my wife for putting up with my obsession with personal finance and investing and for helping me with the layout of this book.

Prologue – Darren, The Average Joe

I grew up in a loving home, in a lower middle-class family. In comparison to those living outside the United States, we were quite wealthy. I always had what I needed, including clothes, shelter and all the food I could eat, but I did not always have what I wanted. In retrospect, I believe this was a good thing.

The first time I remember not having what I wanted was in the 6th grade. I walked into school wearing Tough Skins and a tee-shirt. Tough Skins were blue jeans that had patches sewn or glued onto the knees to keep the fabric from wearing through. Tough Skins were designed for active young boys who like to play hard and as a result destroy their clothes. The tee-shirt I had on was hand-made by my mother to save money. These were nice new clothes that I should have been grateful for, but I was not because they made me the target of ridicule at school by both the other students and even a teacher.

Some of the kids in junior high had designer clothing and none of them wore homemade shirts. As a young boy entering a new world, I felt very insecure and thought that clothing mattered. Most kids wore Levi's 501 jeans and the kids I thought were rich wore Guess clothing. I came home and asked my parents to buy Levi's for me. These bluejeans cost significantly more than my Tough Skins and my mother was not convinced that they would last as long. My parents sat me down and told me that they would always give me what I needed, but would not always be able to afford what I wanted. They suggested that if I wanted to buy things, I should get a job.

I did want to buy things, so I got my first job as a paperboy for the Sacramento Bee. I remember getting up early and folding newspapers so that I could carry them around on my bike and throw them onto the subscribers' porches. If memory serves, I was given a bag that would hold the papers by the Bee. I did not have a bike that was sturdy enough to hold the bag full of papers, so I carried the bag over my head with as many papers as I could and walked the route. It would take two or three trips to deliver all of the papers. My father helped me roll the papers and would drive me around in the car on Sunday because the Sunday papers were full of ads and VERY heavy. It probably would have been easier for him to buy me the 501s, but he was teaching me to work. While my first job did not take too much time, it was a hard job. I had to deliver papers *EVERY* day, even on Christmas! I learned to be responsible. I also learned that I loved getting up early in the morning, riding my bicycle and working. While it was not always fun, I think back with fond memories of my first job.

Eventually, I saved enough money to buy a sturdy enough bike onto which I could mount a rack. I placed a second bag on the rack over the rear wheel of the bicycle. With papers on the rack and over my shoulders, I could complete my route in one trip with the exception of Sunday. I was more efficient due to the purchase of the bike. I didn't realize it at the time but the bike was my first asset. It was what I will call a hard or tangible asset in this book.

I made enough money to buy 501 blue jeans and whatever clothing that I wanted. Once I bought good enough clothing to avoid being teased at school, I stopped spending my money that way. I bought a few other things that I thought I wanted, including a skate board that I never rode much.

The paperboys who had good records of service were entered into drawings to win prizes. I won a dual cassette radio combination, common to the 80s. This was the first bonus that I got from doing a good job. I also learned that if I did a good job and put the papers on the porches of my customers, I would get larger tips. My paper route was more like a business than a job, because I bought the papers from the Bee and sold them to my customers. It was a great life lesson.

The second time I remember not having enough money for what I wanted was when I had an opportunity to go down-hill skiing. Because of the cost, I didn't even bother to ask my parents for the money because I knew that my parents could not pay for it. I also didn't want to spend my hard earned money to slide down a mountain. I had learned the value of a dollar. While I didn't want to spend my money for this activity, it gnawed at me that my parents didn't have enough money to send me on a fun trip. I vowed that when I grew up, I would get a job that would pay enough money to buy what I wanted and allow my future kids to go on fun trips. While this may have not been the best incentive, it did drive me to go to college and study very hard to get an education. I had found the 'why' I describe in Chapter 1 of this book.

Since I didn't spend all of my paper route money, I ended up with excess funds that I didn't know what to do with. My parents suggested that I save my money in a bank account, which I did. I did this for some time, using my money to pay for clothes as they wore out and saving the rest for the future. My savings was my second asset, or what I call a debt or fixed income asset in this book.

One day my brother Troy, who is 10 years my senior, told me that he wanted to buy a house, but did not have enough money for the down payment. I believe it was at my parents urging that he asked me for a loan. Since he said he would pay me more interest than I was earning in the bank, I agreed to do so. Every time he made a payment to me, which he did with diligence until the loan was completely paid off, I wrote down the payment of principal and interest in a green notebook that was set up as a ledger. This was my first experience with accounting, though I didn't know it at the time. I was just keeping track of and counting my money. I also learned that not all assets are created equal: some pay better than others. In giving the bank and my brother a loan, I got my first experience with a debt asset.

I eventually got tired of getting up early and working every single day of the year. When I turned 16, I got my first real job working at a variety store; stocking the shelves and disposing of the trash. It was some time before I was allowed to run the cash register because the manager didn't think I was smart enough to do so. Compared to my job as a paper boy, I worked longer hours, made more money and consequently had to pay taxes at this job. I learned that the government would take its cut of my earnings, which was my first experience with real, unavoidable expenses.

I took physics my senior year of high school and had an excellent teacher, Mr. Craig. I had always loved science, and I was good at math. Our teacher, Mr. Craig, gave us projects to enter into competition with other students. I thoroughly enjoyed using what I had learned in class and applying it to real-life projects. I remember one that day Mr. Craig told us about jobs that use the skills we were learning in physics class. One of them was the job of engineer. He also mentioned that engineers made $31,500 per year on average to start. That sounded like a lot of money to a guy making minimum wage, part-time at a variety store. I vowed that day to become an engineer; in my case a mechanical engineer. I learned that all jobs were not created equal in terms of the salary paid, and that education really matters when it comes to earning a living.

When I graduated from high school, I had saved more than $7,000 for school. This was a sizeable amount at the time, but still not enough to pay for college. I had hoped to get a scholarship to college, but did not score high enough on the college entrance exams to get a four year scholarship. I applied for a scholarship at the only school I wanted to attend; Brigham Young University. I didn't know at the time that there are literally thousands of scholarships available to students who work hard and contribute to their community. However, my parents helped me with college and I was able to finish my first year without having to work and avoiding student loans. This was the only time since I was 11 years old that I didn't have a job. I studied very hard my first year of college and got on the Dean's list. I did well enough my first year to get a scholarship that paid for my second year's tuition. I learned from this experience that hard work is at least as important as intelligence when it comes to being successful in life. I knew that my savings was not enough to last me through 4 years (or in my case 4 ½ years), so I got a part time job as a janitor my second year. I got up at 4 am to clean the same building where some of my engineering courses were held. I never made the Dean's list again while working part time, but I did do well enough to get BYU to pay for half of my tuition for the rest of my stay there. I was grateful for the job, and for the opportunity to get an education.

I thought I had it made when I graduated from college with a Bachelor of Science degree in mechanical engineering. It was 1997 and the economy was booming. Employers were starving for engineers out of college. I was flown around to interviews all over the U.S. and received five offers of employment. I took a position at Hewlett-Packard (HP) where I got to do product design. I had thoroughly enjoyed product design during my senior project at BYU. It turns out that it also paid the most: $44,700 the first year. I thought that I had died and gone to heaven. I had made it to the big time and was ready to enjoy the American dream. My wife and I promptly went out and bought a new car on credit. The monthly payment of principal and interest was $336/month that I paid over 5 long years. This taught me how foolish it was to borrow money to buy things that go down in value. My wife and I were eager to start a family, so we decided also to buy a house for $125,000. The payment was more than $1,200/month, including Private Mortgage Insurance (PMI). We borrowed some money from my parents for the down payment, but it was not enough to reach the 20 percent threshold to avoid PMI. It turns out the house was a much better investment than the car, but it would have been better to save money until we had enough for the 20 percent down payment. I was really into the land of liabilities now. I owed, so off to work I goed.

My wife got pregnant with our first child and quit her job to take care of the baby. With roughly $1,500 in monthly payments, the salary of $44,700 didn't seem so large anymore. Money was very tight. The lack of funds caused contention in my marriage. Money was so tight that we were unable to save for retirement and take advantage of the company match in my 401k. This was crazy, because HP would match the first 3% of my salary that I saved into the 401k. I did get yearly salary increases that were very generous and managed to increase my savings one percent per year until I had the 3 percent match going. I learned about the third type of asset that I will describe in this book, called equity investments. I also joined the stock purchase plan under which HP would buy one share of stock for every two shares that I purchased. I built up a considerable retirement savings in that manner.

I learned, the hard way, that the economy doesn't always boom like it did when I graduated from college. After the 9/11/2001 terrorist attack, the economy took a dive. At the time, I was designing automated cell phone test fixtures for a company called Agilent Technologies, which had split off from HP. The cell phone industry was hit hard by the downturn in the economy and quit buying cell phone test equipment. My job was outsourced to Malaysia. It was cheaper for low-paid workers in Malaysia to test the phones manually than it was to buy and maintain the automated testers that I was designing.

Many at HP had told me that HP doesn't do layoffs, and once you had a job there you were set for life. My head was filled with stories about how the company went to a four day work week to save money instead of resorting to layoffs during previous economic down turns. HP and Agilent did lay off workers this time. Being laid off was hard for me and my family. By this time, we had two kids and no job to support them. It seemed that the world that my parents grew up in, where a person went to work for a company for life and lived on a pension at retirement, was very different from the world I lived in. I lived in a world where people got laid off, worked many different jobs over the course of their careers and were responsible for their own retirement.

I was completely unprepared for the layoff. By the time the layoff occurred, I had upgraded my house and purchased a used truck that I "needed." My wife did not think I needed the truck, and it was another source of contention in our marriage. I had no savings to speak of and a pile of debt that was not getting paid off. Agilent notified me of the layoff four months before I was to exit the company and gave us a generous severance package. I took those four months and consolidated the debt left on my truck by refinancing our new house loan. Fortunately, our first car was paid off by that time. We had reduced our expenses and only had one debt payment; our larger home loan. I was out of work for a month and a half before I landed a temporary job which paid 20 percent less than my job at Agilent. Although the temporary job barely made enough to cover my expenses, I was grateful for the work which got us by while the economy was down.

I eventually found more permanent work at Ball Aerospace. However, it was not as an engineer, but as a Computer Aided Drafting (CAD) technician. I had to swallow my pride and go around installing software for the engineers at Ball. Again, I cannot complain because it was good steady work in a very iffy economy. Part of my job was to teach the engineers how to use the CAD software for which I was responsible. This is where I learned that I really have a gift for teaching. I also found that I was good at diving into software, figuring out how it worked and automating menial tasks by using simple scripting and programming techniques. I learned something more important at Ball than CAD or computer support, however.

I was browsing through the small library that Ball maintained and ran across a book by Robert Kiyosaki. It was called, *Rich Dad's Retire Young, Retire Rich*. This book intrigued me because I was not making much progress toward retirement or any of the visions I had in my head of what it would be like to be a "high income" engineer. I learned that this book was not the first book that Kiyosaki had written on personal finance, so I got his *Rich Dad, Poor Dad* book from the library. I ate that book up. It was simple to understand and taught me the basics of money and personal finance. I highly recommend *Rich Dad, Poor Dad* as it is one of the classics of personal finance. It teaches that personal finance should be treated like a business in order to become wealthy. Reading that book taught me the very basics of accounting and how to manage my own money. More importantly, Kiyosaki's books started me on a quest to learn about money. There was nearly nothing taught in high school about money and very little in the engineering program at BYU. I decided that I needed to learn about money and how it worked in order to reach my goals. Over a period of ten years, I read everything I could get on the subject of personal finance and investing. Some of the information was good, a lot was repetitive, and most was an enormous waste of time. This book is the culmination of my learning and experience in trying to implement the principles I had learned. I write in an effort to let the reader skip all of the bad information that I found and jump right to the good stuff. I hope that I can enlighten you as much as others have helped me on your quest to learn about money. I don't think that I am much different from the average Joe. So if I can do it, then so can you! Follow the principles laid out in the seven chapters of this book and you will become wealthy. It is my firm belief that everyone can achieve their goals in life. Good luck.

WEALTHI – The average Joe's guide to becoming rich

1. *Work*..*2*

2. *Education*..*13*

3. *Accounting*..*23*

4. *Live* Within Your Means...........................*36*

5. *Time* Value of Money..................................*51*

6. *Harvesting Your Efforts*.............................*59*

7. *Insurance and Investing*............................*64*

Appendix A: Recommended Reading

Appendix B: Financial Calculations

Note: The first letter of the title of each chapter of this book spells out the acronym WEALTHI. If you follow the principles outlined in the chapters, you will become wealthy!

Chapter 1 – Why Work hard to become WEALTHI?

The "W" in WEALTHI stands for Work. There is simply no lasting way to build wealth without working hard. It may be possible that one could win the lottery or gain an inheritance from a wealthy relative. However, you are more likely to be hit by lightening than you are to win the lottery. If you don't have some rich uncle who adores you and promises to bequeath his wealth to you, then you will need to work hard to build wealth. Even if you do get an inheritance, you may squander it unless you to learn how to manage your money, and this takes a great deal of work. I'll bet you were seeking the secrets of the rich from this book. The truth is that there are no secrets, just plain common sense steps that require a lot of work in order to become rich.

The "W" in WEALTHI also stands for 'Why'. Why work hard to build wealth? This is the question that we all need to answer for ourselves. If you cannot find out why you want to build wealth, then you have little chance of being successful in the pursuit of becoming wealthy. Typically, in order to make a change, you need to associate more pain with **not** changing than you associate with changing. This principle is taught in a book called *The Seven Habits of Highly Effective People* written by the late Dr. Steven Covey. I highly recommend this book.

What is your reason? Why do you want to build wealth? Where is the pain in your life? Do you want to be able to retire and play the recreational sport of your choosing? Do you want to build a nice house on acreage where you can be alone and pursue your interests? Do you want to be free from having a job and answering to a boss? Do you want to say goodbye to your customers and be free from having the phone ring all of the time? Do you want to quit your job and move to a retirement community where you can socialize with people in a similar station in life? Do you want to ride on cruise ships and see the world? You must have a reason, and a good reason, in order to do what it takes to become wealthy. I get the most satisfaction from doing charitable work, especialy teaching, but charitable activities don't pay very well and I have a large family to support. I **really** don't like being told what to do, and I **really, really** don't like being told how to do what I have been asked to do. I get my reason to build wealth from my desire to do what I want with my time and doing it the way that I want to do it. I also want to be able to pay for my children's college tuition and travel with my wife when I get older. All of these goals require money and are the driving force for me to follow the principles of this book.

Consider the story of a young man who wants to become wealthy. We'll call him Joe. He seeks out a mentor; an older gentleman who owns several successful businesses. We'll call him Bill. Joe pleads with Bill to tell him the secrets of being rich. Bill does not have time for Joe, so he blows Joe off several times. Finally, Joe convinces Bill to have lunch with him. At lunch, Bill tries to determine if Joe really wants to be rich. After much cajoling, Joe manages to get Bill to give him one lesson. Bill wants Joe to meet him at the top of one of his apartment buidlings. Joe shows up in his best business suit. After admiring the view, Bill grabs joe by the lapels of his suit and holds him over the edge of the building and says, "Do you really want to be rich?" Joe answers, "Yes, but please pull me back from the edge." Bill responds, "When you want to be rich as much as you want to come back from the edge, you will be ready to learn from me." Joe left after this encounter and did not ask Bill for further advice, but the experience stuck with him. This is an extreme example, but you get my point. If you really want it, you can become rich, but it will take hard work, sacrifice and perhaps some risk taking.

Why do you want to become wealthy? If you don't have a reason, I suggest you put this book down and ponder your reasons for a minute or a week. If you don't have a good reason, then you need to get one before you embark on trying to do the rest of the things I suggest in this book because they require work. You also need to associate pain with not getting what you want. You need to truly believe that a relatively short duration of pain will be better than a long life of dull pain ending only in a death preceded by the realization that you could've done more, been more, and helped more people. Your "Why" needs to be so emotional that it causes you to tear up when you think about it. Get your "Why" now and write it down in the space provided on the next page.

Why I want to be WEALTHI:

_____

_____

_____

_____

_____

_____

_____

_____

_____

_____

_____

_____

_____

_____

_____

_____

_____

Work is a natural law of the universe and always has been. Genesis 3:19 of the King James version of the Holy Bible states, "In the sweat of thy face shalt thou eat bread, till thou return unto the ground." All people are required to work in order to survive on this planet. If you do not believe me, then just stop working for a while (which is a good way to determine how wealthy you really are). You might think that you can live on welfare or some other charitable subsistance. This may be possible, but it is not fun and still requires a bit of work to get money from government agencies. You may be the recipient of a large inheritance that can support you for a long time. However, wealth requires effort and the wisdom to care for it. Most wealth disappears in one generation if the inheritors are not taught how to preserve it and work at doing so.

Building wealth is not easy, but can be done by following the principles taught in this book. Becoming wealthy requires discipline and hard work. Work is not the end all for building wealth, but it is the start, and one cannot build wealth without work. If you are looking for a get rich quick scheme then you have picked the wrong book. I'm not going to tell you to buy tons of real estate with nothing down or risk your savings on derivatives in the stock market. I am going to describe how the vast majority of wealthy people in the United States have built their wealth.

So how does one work hard? Working hard is very simple, but takes discipline. When you have a job, do the work you have been asked to do. When you own a business then make sure you are providing a quality product or service at a reasonable price. Do not spend time goofing off with co-workers, surfing the internet or figuring out how to scam your customers out of their money. You might be able to do these activities for a while, but they will come back to haunt you. Employers will realize who their best employees are, and customers will learn that they can get a better deal elsewhere. This principle is tightly related to the principle explained in Chapter 6, "Harvesting Your Efforts". You will reap what you sow, and if you sow hard work you will reap the benefits.

I had a co-worker (yes, the critical word there is "had"). I'll call him Bob. He always seemed to be away from his desk. He is a very social person, so I supposed he spent some of this time talking to others around the work place. One day we had a surprise fire drill and Bob was no where to be found. Bob got into a bit of trouble when he couldn't be located. If this were a real fire and we couldn't find Bob, then the fire fighters would have to go in and look for him. When my manager asked Bob where he was during the fire drill, he said that he was out back having a smoke. This was clearly a lie since everyone who was present at the fire drill was out back waiting for the drill to be over. Bob then said that he must have been in his car listening to the radio while smoking and didn't see everyone congregating outside. This was also clearly a lie as we were all out back in the parking lot in plain view of anyone sitting in his car listening to the radio. In fact, he had gone off site and lied about where he was. He was terminated within a month of this incident. I cannot stress the importance of working hard at whatever it is you do. It is also critical to have Integrity. If you're not putting in a day's work for a day's pay, then I suggest you correct the situation immediately. Read more about this in Chapter 6, "Harvesting Your Efforts."

My mother taught me a sound principle when I was very young; do a little more than your employer or customers ask of you. This book will be worth every penny you spent on it if you follow this simple guidance. When you do a little extra, you will be set apart from the other employees or your competitors. I suggest that you spend an extra hour at work everyday. Come in to work half an hour early and leave half an hour later than you are required to do. This benefits you in two ways. 1) Your employers will see that you are putting forth extra effort, or your customers will get access to your products or services a little bit longer. 2) You will have time to do things that not only get more work done, but also improve your productivity and the productivity of others around you. This extra hour per day will not only help you with your job, likely leading to larger pay raises and promotions, but it will also give you time to work on skills or tools that will make you more productive. Even if you don't see immediate financial benefits from working harder, you will learn the discipline required to become wealthy.

I have had employers who have preached the virtues of a family-friendly workplace and work/life balance. These same people have never complained when I have put in extra time or done something extra. Let me tell you a little secret: Employers and customers like hard workers whether they say so or not. I learned this principle the hard way. When I got my first job out of college there was a very tight market for mechanical engineers. I ended up with 5 offers from employers and got to choose where I would be employed. The favorable position I was in was due in part to the booming economy, but also to the hard work I put into my schooling. I thought that my services were highly valued, and I was determined not to work a minute more than eight hours per day. I was arrogant and had to learn a hard lesson. Another person was hired at almost the same time that I was. She worked very hard and spent more than an extra hour at work every day. Pretty soon it was evident that she was getting all of the interesting work and I was not. It was not long before she was promoted. I had to change jobs and show my new boss that I was willing to work hard and give a little more than asked before getting the big raises and promotions.

Now, I'm not saying be a work-a-holic. There is no joy in life if you spend it all at work. What I am suggesting is that you give up an hour of TV or an hour of video game playing or even an hour of sleep to put in a little extra at work. It will pay off, perhaps not in the first week, but it will likely pay off in the first year. You will get a larger raise or a promotion when the boss realizes your commitment to the company or your customers realize your commitment to providing quality products and services.

It may be that you work for an hourly wage or work a shift and it is impossible or very difficult to work an extra hour a day. If this is the case, then it is likely that you make a low wage and you need to read Chapter 2 of this book. There are other, better things that you can do with your extra time, such as; studying what you need to study in order to become better at your job or getting an advanced degree that will qualify you for a better paying job, tracking your finances, or studying personal finance and investing. All will reap great rewards on your path to becoming wealthy. Give up an hour of television, an hour of surfing the internet or an hour of video games and you will feel better about yourself. This may seem like a sacrifice at first. My definition of sacrifice comes from Reed Benson, a professor I had at BYU. He said, "Sacrifice is giving up something good, for something better." Surely you will be glad to give up an extra hour of work each day for better pay, a sense of accomplishment and better control over your financial life. If all of this seems like too much work then you need to go back and revisit your "Why." Make sure you have a solid reason to do the things I describe here and write that reason down.

Even if you do work an extra hour a day, I also suggest that you spend your extra hour doing things that will make you more productive. In Chapter 2 – "Education," I suggest that you get all of the education you can in your chosen profession. The extra hour is a great time to spend studying for a degree. If you don't want to pursue a degree, then why not spend an hour studying the tasks you perform each day and work on ways to do them faster or more efficiently? What if you spent time developing a new process, researching a new tool or devising a better way to get your job done? If you draw upon your creative intelligence, I'll bet that you can find ways to get your job done better. Even if all you do is work an extra hour doing what you normally do, the benefits will be evident. In Steven Covey's book, *The 7 Habits of Highly Effective People,* the habit that I just described is habit number seven called "Sharpen the Saw," or improving your "Production Capacity." We need to spend time getting better at what we do, not only doing more of it.

I also recommend the book *The Millionaire Next Door* by Stanley & Denko, which explains that millionaires, those especially good at building wealth, work on average 45 - 50 hours per week. These people are not work-a-holics, but they do recognize the need to do a little more than average in order to get ahead in life. The best way to learn how to build wealth is to study, interview, and document your findings from those people who have wealth, especially those who have gained their wealth through their own efforts. This is what Stanley and Denko did. Get *The Millionaire Next Door*. Read it and re-read it. My copy is ear-marked and highlighted so that I can review the important quotations in a single sitting.

The bottom line is this: work is required in order to become wealthy. Wealth is not found at the casino, in line for lottery tickets or by following get rich quick schemes. I ask you to test the principle of working an extra hour everyday for a year and see if you do not reap worthwhile benefits. I also challenge you to spend an extra hour of the workday improving your production capacity. This could involve reading a book on personal finance (like you are right now), exercising, planning your day, planning your future and setting goals, tracking your finances or a number of other things that are too many to mention. Use your creative intelligence to come up with what you will do to improve your own situation. If you are a religious person, then ask God what your time will be best used for, and He will guide you to do what will make the most difference in not only your life, but in the lives of those around you. I know that this is not easy, but it will be worth it. I am working hard to write this book because I believe that it will not only make me wealthy, but because I believe there is a real need in the world for the knowledge that I have gained by reading, studying and applying the principles taught in this book. These topics are not taught in school, and are generally not taught in college, but they are taught in books like this one. Read this book and the others that I recommend in this book and implement the things you learn. You will not be sorry, but you will become wealthy in more ways than one. Winners Work Hard to become WEALTHI. It is not the smartest, the fastest or the most attractive people who build wealth (though those qualities don't hurt). It is those who have the discipline to work hard and sacrifice. Read on to find out what else it takes.

For help with getting inspired to do what it takes to become wealthy, I recommend *On Fire: The 7 Choices to Ignite a Radically Inspired Life*, by John O'Leary. O'Leary's book has inspired me to finish my book.

Chapter 2 – Education

The "E" in WEALTHI stands for Education. This chapter is designed to show you that all work is not created equal. There is a wide disparity between what people in the United States get paid for their work. Doctors get paid large sums of money for the knowledge and skill they have acquired. Business leaders get paid outrageous amounts of money for leading large companies. Others work and toil hard their entire lives for little pay or benefit. Much of the disparity can be explained by hard work, but there is more to it than work. Education has a significant effect on the amount of money that one earns over the course of a lifetime.

So, what is the average income of families in the United States? The government did a survey in 2010 that listed the average pretax household income as approximately $75,000. This may seem like a lot of money to many people. The interesting thing is that the median pretax income for Americans was listed by the Census ACS survey as $53,637 in 2014. This is not a lot of money and could be considered to be the poverty level in some very expensive places like New York City or San Francisco. The median simply means the middle number when there are an odd number of numbers. When there is an even number of numbers then the median is the average of the two middle numbers. There were exactly half the families who made more and half the families who made less in 2014 than $53,637. Why the discrepancy between the average and the median? The answer is that there are a relatively few number of families that make very large amounts of money and skew the average up. Take the following list of numbers as an example:

1   2   2   2   2   3   4   5   9   1   20   60

The median of these numbers is 3.5. The average of these numbers is 10. So, what does it take to earn more than the average, or even the median salary??? What does it take to be on the right side of the graph or the right side of the income earners in America? The answer, in large part, is education. The same study shows income by education level of the head of the household. See the graph below. Take a close look at the data and let it sink in.

Education	Average Income	Median Income
No High School	$31,300.00	$22,200.00
High School Diploma	$51,100.00	$36,700.00
Some College	$68,100.00	$45,600.00
College Degree	$143,800.00	$78,200.00

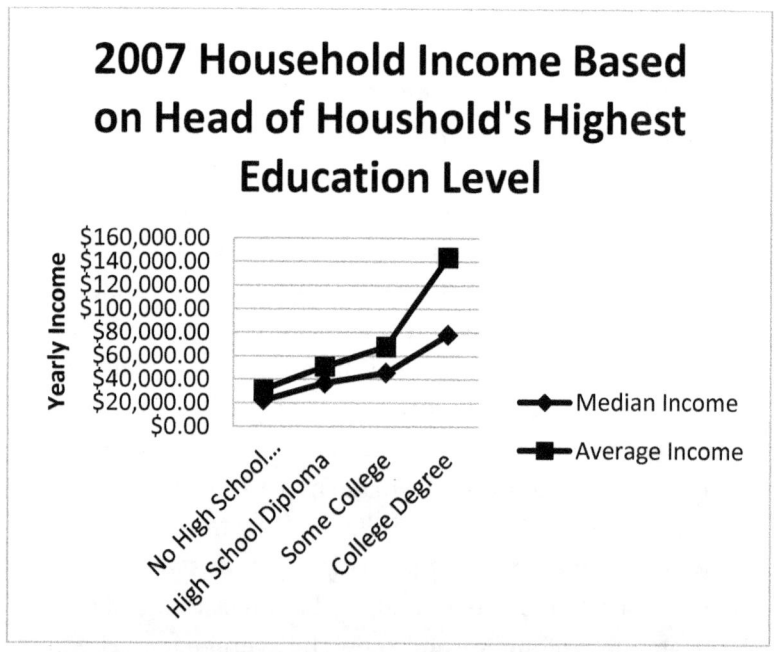

The people who have a college degree make significantly more money that those who do not. I wish that someone would've shown this data to me before leaving high school.

I'm grateful that my family stressed the importance of getting a college degree even though I did not have this data. That is not to say that a college degree will guarantee that you make at least the average income. It is also not required to have a college degree in order to earn the average income. It is to say that you are *likely* to earn more if you have a college degree than if you don't. With that said, not all degrees are created equal. The chart below shows the median income of people in the specified occupations.

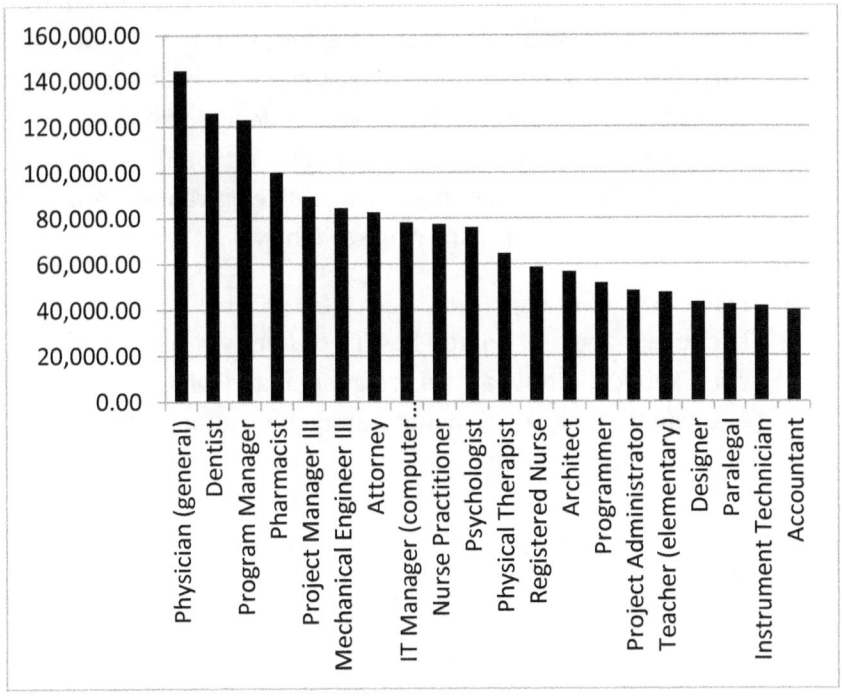

Note that many of the higher income occupations are in the medical field. It should also be noted that many of the professions listed require working with or managing people. People skills are highly valued. Most, if not all, of these occupations require a college degree and all require special skills.

Why not get a college degree to help increase your income? Here is a list of excuses that I have heard and come across.

Top Excuses for Not Getting an Education

1. *I did poorly in school.*

   While it is true that the top colleges require good grades and test scores on college entrance exams, there are many schools that do not. In fact, junior colleges typically only require a fee to take a class. If you did poorly in high school, you can go to junior college, work very hard (see Chapter 1 of this book) and earn grades that are good enough to transfer to a four year school. Contact the university that you have your eye on and see which junior colleges have classes that meet the entry requirements of the four year school. It may surprise you that it is much easier to get into a four year college with an appropriate associates degree from and accredited junior college than it is to be accepted as a freshman directly out of high school. The entrance exam may also be waived for transferring students.

2. *I'm not smart enough.*

   I believe that every person has his or her own significant gifts. Think about what you are good at and what others have told you that you excel in and pursue education or training in this area. I think most people are capable of obtaining a four year degree in an area in which they are gifted, but college isn't for everyone. Even if you cannot stand the idea of attending a four year college, make sure you get some post high school training. There are technical training institutions and journeyman paths that teach critical skills for increasing one's earning potential. As I've already demonstrated, those with an education or training in a field make more than those who don't.

3. *College costs too much money.*

   There is some validity to this statement. Universities value the services they provide, especially the top so called "Ivy League" institutions. However, the fact of the matter is that schools that are funded by federal and state governments teach the exact same things that the top universities teach and do it for much lower tuition rates. In fact, in some states, college tuition is free if the student's high school grades are high enough. One of my friends in high school was very talented both academically and physically. She applied to and was accepted at Stanford University. However, the tuition at Stanford was prohibitive and she didn't want to pile up hundreds of thousands of dollars in debt to attend that prestigious school. She was also accepted at Utah State University and got a full ride scholarship that allowed her to graduate with no debt. Being successful has much more to do with how hard you work and study in school than does the name of the school you attended (see Chapter 1). In addition to academic and athletic scholarships, there are thousands of scholarships available to recently graduated students who have worked and served in their communities. Do an internet search and, if necessary, pay a small fee for a list of scholarships. A summer spent searching and applying for scholarships may pay large dividends. Don't apply for just a few scholarships either. Apply for hundreds of scholarships. Many of the requirements for a scholarship application are the same, so the amount of work required for each additional application gets smaller as the number of applications increases. The U.S. military will also pay for schooling if the graduate agrees to serve for several years after graduation. The military is not for everyone, but if it is suitable for you it is an option worth looking into. There are also companies willing to pay for tuition while you work for them full or even part time. UPS is one example of a company that will pay for tuition if you agree to work 20 hours per week during college. There are even scholarships targeted specifically at "returning students," or adults looking to complete a degree program started earlier in life or to start a new degree later in life.

4. *College takes too long.*

    You might think that you need to get into the workforce and
    start earning money now! If you waste two to ten years in
    college, then you have wasted time you could have been
    earning, saving and investing your money. Time sacrificed to
    get an education yields sharply increased income over a
    lifetime. Consider the following example.

Occupation	# of Years Worked Before Age 65	Income/Year	Income/Life
Entry Level	47	$20,000.00	$940,000.00
Mechanical Engineer III	43	$84,377.00	$3,628,211.00
Dentist	40	125,952.00	$5,038,080.00

    While the dentist spends 7 more years in college than the
    entry level person, he makes over five times as much over
    the course of his career.

5. *I'm too old to get an education.*

    Age will definitely have an impact on your analysis explained
    in "College takes too long," above. However, it is getting more
    and more common for older individuals to get college
    degrees. Many online accredited institutions offer flexible
    classes for working adults. Many other traditional brick and
    mortar schools offer evening and weekend classes in
    addition to online courses for working professionals. If the
    company you work for does not reimburse for tuition, then
    consider switching companies, especially if you do not have
    any post high school education.

    If you are willing to work hard and get an education related
    to your chosen profession, you will be on your way to

becoming wealthy. What if you simply can't stand the idea of going to school for a post high school education? When I was graduating high school, my older brother gave me some wise counsel. He said that I should choose a profession that either:

1) Other people can't do or

2) Other people won't do.

An example of the first type is the professional athlete or artist. An example of the second type is the salesman. A combination of both 1) and 2) are typically the highest paying careers. These people might be star athletes who start business after retiring from their chosen sport, or corporate CEOs. This typically requires a large amount of education and business acumen. CEOs of large corporations typically have a Master's in Business Administration (MBA) degree and many years of proven business successes and are gifted at leading people. I don't recommend pursuing the first type of profession unless you are significantly gifted. Your gifts should be evidenced by other people giving you awards or by you having won many competitions. The second type of profession may be worth considering if you cannot stand the idea of college and you have good people skills.

Sales

Are you a popular person who is good at influencing others to your way of thinking? Then sales may be right for you. Even if you are not particularly gregarious, sales skills can be learned with practice. When you come to think of it, every product or service that is consumed must be sold in one way or another. Every business that exists needs salespeople to push their goods or services. Businesses pay very well for salespeople who can move their merchandise. This is a profession that requires a thick skin and a tolerance for rejection. There are different types of intelligence and the sales profession is one that requires an emotional intelligence. The ability to control one's emotions in response to the feedback from others is critical in this area. I am not a salesman and cannot begin to claim expertise in this area. I will leave a description of how to be a great salesman to the many other books on the topic. What I do know is that good salespeople are in high demand and are very highly compensated. Sales is a field where one can make a six figure salary without needing a formal education. Good sales skills are also required in order to be an entrepreneur as an entrepreneur's first job is to generate revenue for his company. Generating revenue starts with the sale. I would highly recommend trying out the sales profession before embarking on entrepreneurship.

Entrepreneur

In my quest to learn about becoming wealthy, it has become clear that the best way to become extremely wealthy is to start your own business. I'm sure some names of the wealthiest people in the world come to mind: Bill Gates, Warren Buffet, etc. The list of people who have become extremely wealthy by starting their own businesses is too long to include here. Although being an entrepreneur may not require a formal training, it is one of the most difficult and competitive occupations out there. Take a look at the graph below of people who are "self employed" vs. those who work for someone else.

	Median Income	Average Income
Head of Household Works for Someone Else	56,600.00	83,100.00
Head of Household is Self-Employed	75,700.00	191,800.00

Those who work for themselves earn one third more than those working for someone else. This table also sheds light on how the median and average income of households in general are brought down by people who are retired and/or not working. This data is also backed up by the book, *The Millionaire Next Door* which claims that 2/3 of all millionaires are small business owners. It is not required to own a small business to be a millionaire, but it is definitely a good path to follow on your quest to build wealth.

These tables do not show the risk that entrepreneurs take on. I'm sure that you have heard that most small businesses fail within their first 5 years. There can be a great deal of investment required to start an entrepreneurial endeavor. When the business fails, the money is gone, leaving the aspiring entrepreneur with significant losses, a great deal of debt or some very disappointed investors. At the very least, the self-employed individual needs to be able to survive on a limited or non-existent salary while the business gets on its feet. While there is a great deal of risk in starting up an enterprise, some believe that the risks are worth the reward, so they try many times to start a new business (and sometimes declare bankruptcy many times) before becoming successful. Being an entrepreneur is perhaps the most risky and least diversified way to invest your own money because not only is your capital at risk, but your income is as well. I write more on investing in Chapter 7, "Insurance and Investing."

Chapter 3 – Accounting

The "A" in WEALTHI stands for Accounting. I know that most of you are rolling your eyes or thinking of skipping to the next chapter simply based on the title of this one. Don't! Accounting is not hard, especially the type of personal accounting that I will discuss in this chapter.

Accounting = Arithmetic + Counting

Some accountants may get offended by this equation. I realize that there is a lot more to corporate accounting than is described in this simplified equation. The government has made sure that the job of the professional accountant is a very difficult one. However, it is not difficult to be your own personal accountant. Believe it or not, the most difficult math that you will have to do in order to be your own personal accountant is arithmetic. Most of personal accounting is simply counting up what you earn and save and subtracting what you spend and owe. It is that simple.

Think of the accountant as a score keeper. How much fun would it be to watch a baseball, basketball or football game without knowing what the score is? I can just see it now: what a great play, but who's winning? I can't remember without a scorekeeper. If you don't keep track of your own personal finances, then not only will you not know if you are becoming wealthy, but you will not know if you can even pay your bills. If you do keep track of your finances, you will be able to know if you are winning the game of money. There will be a great peace that comes over you when you know where your next mortgage payment is coming from and how you will be able to retire.

How do you know if you are winning the game or have won altogether? I submit that you have won the game when your income surpasses your expenses, without you having to work. This of course does not mean that you must stop working, only that you don't have to work any longer.

There are two basic personal accounting scorecards; the cash flow statement and the balance sheet. The cash flow statement, otherwise known as an income statement is like the score card. (In real accounting the cash flow and income statements are actually very different, but for our purposes we will treat them the same.) The balance sheet yields your "net worth" and is like your record of wins and losses. Take a look at a simple personal cash flow statement below. I recommend keeping a cash flow statement on a monthly basis. While it is possible to do this more frequently, most bills are due on a monthly basis and I don't want all of the free spirits out there bogged down by accounting multiple times a month!

Cash Flow Statement

Take the time, right now, to fill out the cash flow statement on the next page. If you have some income or expenses that do not fit into the categories listed then fill them in the "Other" lines. Add up your income and your expenses and subtract the latter from the former. If you have never done this then now is the time! This is why I have provided space to do this in this book. It is critical to you becoming wealthy for you to track your income and expenses.

INCOME

EARNED INCOME FROM YOUR JOB #1 _____

EARNED INCOME FROM YOUR JOB #2 _____

INTEREST _____

DIVIDENDS _____

BUSINESS INCOME _____

CAPITAL GAINS _____

OTHER INCOME _____

TOTAL INCOME _____

EXPENSES

TITHING OR CHARITABLE DONATIONS _____

TAXES _____

HOUSING (RENT OR MORTGAGE PAYMENT) _____

TRANSPORTATION (GAS, CAR PAYMENT, MAINTENANCE) _____

FOOD (PREPARED AT HOME) _____

FOOD (EATING OUT) _____

CLOTHING _____

UTILITIES _____

ENTERTAINMENT _____

INSURANCE (HEALTH, AUTOMOTIVE, LIFE, ETC.) _____

OTHER EXPENSE _____

TOTAL EXPENSES _____

CASH FLOW = TOTAL INCOME – TOTAL EXPENSES _____

Accounting

I have listed some categories for the cash flow statement. In order to figure out if you are winning the game then list all of your income sources and sum them up. Then list out all of your monthly expenses and sum them up. Subtract the expenses from the income and you will get your cash flow. Here is an example to get you started.

INCOME - EXPENSES = CASH FLOW

Monthly Cash Flow
Spreadsheet Example

	Monthly Amount	Notes
Income		
Spouse #1	$4,166.67	$50,000.00/year
Spouse #2	$2,083.33	$25,000.00/year
Interest on savings	$75.00	
Total Income	$6,325.00	
Expenses		
Charitable Giving	$632.50	10% of income
Taxes (Federal, State, Social Security, Medicare)	$1,581.25	25% of income
Mortgage Payment	$1,500.00	
Insurance (Auto, Home Owner's, Health)	$500.00	Health Insurance
Food	$500.00	
Clothing	$150.00	
Utilities	$150.00	
Cell Phones	$100.00	
Internet	$50.00	
Gas/Car Maintenance	$112.00	
Spending money	$100.00	
Total Expenses	$5,363.75	
Cash Flow = Income - Expenses	**$949.25**	
Investing		
401k Contributions	**$949.25**	~15% of income

The above example is somewhat of an ideal budget. The idea here is to minimize expenses and maximize income, so that there is cash flow to invest. Don't be frustrated if yours does not look this free of expenses or have this large percentage of income going to investing. Chapter 4, "Live Within Your Means," will help you improve your cash flow statement.

If you get a positive cash flow, then you are ahead of the game. If you get a negative cash flow, then you need to take a close look at the expenses to see if there is something you can trim. This is like the home team vs. the visitors. The home team needs to be winning if you are to become WEALTHI. This exercise may seem very basic to some of you. However, the vast majority of people I have worked with have not completed the simple task of creating a cash flow statement. If you haven't created your own cash flow statement, then do so now! I cannot stress enough the importance of keeping score in this way. A positive cash flow is the basic requirement to becoming wealthy. A negative number at the bottom of your cash flow statement not only means you are losing the game, but probably that you are going into debt. One of the latest business buzz words is "sustainability." I don't use the new meaning of this word that has to do with environmental concerns, but the old one that relates to whether or not a person can sustain their standard of living. I can guarantee that if you have a negative number at the bottom of your cash flow statement that your finances are NOT sustainable. If you have a negative number at the bottom of the cash flow statement then you need to fix the problem immediately. I'll discuss ways to do this in the Chapter 4, "Live Within Your Means." I'll discuss what to do with the benefits of having a positive cash flow in Chapter 7, "Insurance and Investing."

Children have a need to test the limits that their parents give to them. They will push and push until the parents create consequences. My youngest son is in the process of testing these limits with his parents as I write this book. I am no great parent, by any means, but I have used a technique with him that seems to work. He loves to be independent, a big boy. When he is misbehaving I use the phrase, "We can do it the hard way, or the easy way." Now, before you all call social services, I need to describe what I mean by this statement. The hard way is for Dad to help him do what he needs to do. The easy way is for him to do it by himself. An example is putting on his shoes. He feels great when he can do it himself, but sometimes he refuses and Dad has to help.

There is a little bit of the 3 year old in all of us. We don't want to do a cash flow statement because it is not fun (unless you are a complete finance geek like me). Unfortunately, we will do it the easy way or the hard way. The hard way might involve having the power turned off, getting evicted or sitting down with a bankruptcy attorney. I guarantee that it is more fun to do your finances the easy way.

If you just can't imagine spending time to create a cash flow statement then try this simple step. Keep a small notebook in your pocket and write down all the things you spend money on for one day. You'll be amazed at where your money goes. Keep track of your money for one week this same way. Again, you will be amazed. Do this for a month and you are on your way to creating a cash flow statement. Once you have done it for a month, you can make a plan for the next month. This plan is called a budget and it tells your money where to go for the next month. Sit down with your spouse, if you have one, and plan out where you are going to spend your money for the next month. You will see things that disgust you and places to trim back that will help you save money. Keep track of your spending for another month and you can compare it to your budget. This simple act usually creates incentive to save and tell your money where to go. It usually requires about three months to get your cash flow statement under control and live within your budget.

Balance Sheet

The second score card you need to put together is the balance sheet, or your personal net worth statement. This score card will tell you if you are building wealth and how your assets and liabilities are treating you. Once you have learned how to keep score on a short term monthly basis, it is a good idea to take snapshots in time over longer periods, like every year. Before we embark on the balance sheet, we need to define two important terms: Asset and Liability. Again, don't let these accounting terms scare you. I will simplify them as follows.

An asset is anything that has a marketable value. In other words an asset is anything that you can sell for money and has a market containing people willing to buy it. Common examples of assets are stocks and bonds. However, the clothes in your closet or your washing machine are assets if you can sell them on eBay, Craigslist or the newspaper. With that said, not all assets are created equal. There are good assets and bad assets.

Good assets tend to go up in value, pay you money or eliminate expenses. An example of a good asset is a stock that pays a dividend or trends up in value. Another example is a Certificate of Deposit (CD) which pays interest. A house can be a good or a bad asset, depending on whether it is going up or down in value, how much maintenance is required and whether or not you can afford it. An example of a bad asset is a car that is not used for business purposes. Why is this, you ask? Cars, and just about anything with a motor, typically go down in value. In fact, a new car typically loses 1/5 of its value when you drive it off the lot. You may come to think that I hate cars after reading this book. I assure you that I don't hate cars; I have just learned that they can destroy a person's ability to create wealth.

Liabilities are obligations that you have to another party. I remember the meaning of this word by thinking that liabilities give you the 'ability' to 'lie' about how wealthy you are. Typically, liabilities are debts or money that you owe other people. It is fairly easy in today's economy to go into debt to buy just about anything. Common examples are mortgages on houses, loans on cars, credit card balances, personal bank loans and the worst of all, payday or consignment loans. We can take on liabilities to buy things that make us look wealthy. However, liabilities simply turn us into slaves to our stuff. In Proverbs 22:7 it states, "The rich ruleth over the poor and the borrower is servant to the lender." These words are very true. When we borrow from others we become their servants. One of the goals of this book is to help you become debt free. Getting out of debt is a great way to build wealth because it opens up your income to invest in assets. I will discuss this more in Chapter 4, "Live Within Your Means."

But, you say, it is impossible to become debt free in today's society!

It is hard to get out of debt, but not impossible. Becoming debt free requires a person to live beneath his means and obey the law of the harvest (see Chapter 6, "Harvest Your Efforts"). Becoming debt free requires sacrifice and self-discipline. In this case it means living beneath your means today so that you can be free tomorrow. I'll provide more on how to get out of debt later.

Here is the equation for your net worth.

$$ASSETS - LIABILITIES = NET\ WORTH$$

Accounting

Again, the math is quite simple. Add up everything that you own and subtract every that you owe and you will come up with your net worth. If this is a positive number then you have some wealth. If it is negative or zero then you are BROKE. Being broke is not the same as being poor. Being poor is a state of mind and being broke simply means you don't have any assets right now. This book will tell you how to acquire assets. Create your balance sheet right now! Now is the time to see how you are doing in the game of money. If the space provided on the next page is not adequate for your balance sheet, then use the space provided below, another sheet of paper or use a spread sheet, like I do.

Assets

401k #1 _____

401k #2 _____

IRA #1 _____

IRA #2 _____

Checking Account _____

Savings Account _____

Value of Home _____

Value of Investment property _____

Total Value of Cars _____

Other Asset _____

TOTAL ASSETS _____

Liabilities

Home Mortgage #1 _____

Home Mortgage #2 _____

Car Loan #1 _____

Car Loan #2 _____

Credit Card Debt _____

Retail Debt (i.e. Furniture) _____

Medical Debt _____

Other Liabililty _____

TOTAL Liabilities

NET WORTH = TOTAL ASSETS – TOTAL LIABILITIES _____

Balance Sheet Example

<u>Assets</u>

House	$276,000.00
Emergency Fund (Money Market Account)	$30,000.00
401k #1	$250,000.00
401k #2	$125,000.00
Total Assets	<u>$681,000.00</u>

<u>Liabilities</u>

1st Home Mortgage	$220,800.00
Outstanding Credit Card Bills	$1,500.00
Total Liabilities	<u>$222,300.00</u>

Net Worth = Assets - Liabilities   **<u>$458,700.00</u>**

This is also a very good balance sheet with limited liabilities. Don't be frustrated if your net worth is not this big. Remember, you need to know what the score is before you can win the game of money. The idea here is to pay off your liabilities so that you can use your cash flow to buy assets. I suggest that you create a balance sheet right now, using the form that I provided or your own spreadsheet, so that you know where you are in the game of money. I also find it enlightening to tally up all of the interest you are paying on your debts. See how to eliminate your debt in the next chapter.

Chapter 4 – Live Within Your Means

The "L" in WEALTHI stands for "Live" Within Your Means. While in a doctor's office a few years ago, I read an article about a young couple who had recently immigrated to the United States. They were thrilled to have moved to such a wealthy country where they could have whatever they wanted by buying it on credit. When living in their old country, they were forced to buy everything with cash because credit was not available. First, they bought a television for $350 on credit. Then they bought an automobile on credit and eventually a house, you guessed it, on credit. I remember thinking to myself that their banker must really love these people. They had really embraced the culture of America. Get whatever you want NOW and pay for it the rest of your life. I was disgusted with the article because the author did not point out the folly of their actions and, in fact, thought it was a great plan. The sad truth is that most people live their lives this way; constantly paying the banker for items bought on credit.

Let's consider exactly how much the immigrant; I'll call him Joe, paid for his lack of patience. If he paid for his TV with a credit card at 14% interest (the average interest rate that credit cards charge) with a required 2% minimum payment and a $10 absolute minimum payment, it would take him 3 years, 10 months and $450 dollars. Recent credit card laws require credit card companies to show the borrower how long it will take to pay off items purchased on credit based on minimum payments. You can find this information on your credit card bill.

How long would it have taken him to save for a television if he put $10 into a money market account that earned them an average of 4 percent per year? (Current money market rates may be higher or lower than at the writing of this book.) The answer is 2 years, 9 months and about $330 dollars. Joe would've saved $120 and a year of being in debt. Not only that, but he would've had extra time, not spent watching TV, to read great books like this one that could help him avoid a life of bondage! This type of finance method is called a sinking fund by finance types. I recommend a sinking fund to save for consumer items. Let's review the purchase. Note that the 4% goes into Joe's pocket while the 14% comes out of his pocket.

Finance Method	TV Cost	Interest	Payoff Time	Total Cost
Credit Card 14%	$350	$100	46 Months	$450
Sinking Fund (4%)	$350	($20)	34 Months	$330
		Savings By Saving	12 Months	**$120**

The other detail that should be mentioned here is that when you save for a consumer item, you learn what the real cost is BEFORE the purchase is made. This has a tendency to cause the buyer to spend less, perhaps buying a less expensive TV in this case. In fact, the TV would have cost less 3 years later as electronics tend to get better and cost less over time. The TV purchase on credit alone would not break Joe financially. The problem is that the TV experience got them hooked on credit and caused them to continually finance their banker's lifestyle. The problems only get worse as the size of the debt increases.

Live Within Your Means

So let's look at buying a new, inexpensive car for $20,000. Assuming a 5 year loan and a 7 percent interest rate (the current average going rate), their payment would be $392.02/month for 60 months. How much did Joe spend for his car that drops in value the minute he drives off the lot? The math here is easier. $392.02 X 60 = $23,761.44. They paid their banker $3,761.44 for the privilege of having the new car smell and watching the car go down in value. How much would they have saved if they had patiently put away money for the car? If they put $392.02 per month into the previously mentioned money market account at 4 percent, they would've had their new car in 47 months or just under 4 years and it would've cost them only $18,501.32. The bottom line in this deal is that they spent an extra $5,260 and an extra year of their lives for the new car smell. Let's review again.

Finance Method	Car Cost	Interest	Payoff Time	Total Cost
Auto Loan 7%	$20,000	$3,761	60 Months	$23,761
Sinking Fund 4%	$20,000	($1,499)	47 Months	$18,501
		Savings By Saving	13 Months	$5,260

Think of it this way, they drove around in their new car and threw a $100 dollar bill out the window every month for more than 4 years. Do you have that kind of money to blow? Do you have five grand that you would like to give to your local or not so local banker? Hundreds of thousands of people do this all the time. I was one of them and I bet you are too. None of this takes into account the fact that a new car depreciates extremely fast in the first 3 years of ownership. It is much less expensive to buy a car that is 1 to 3 years old and has already dropped in price significantly from the new price of the car. My advice is to wait and save for 3 years and then buy a slightly used car and a can of new car smell that you can get at your local automotive store for $9.99.

What does Joe do while he is saving up money to buy a car? Walk, ride the bus or his bicycle, join a car/vanpool or buy an old car for $2,000 or less while he saves up to buy a better car.

If that was shocking to you, then hold on to your hat. Let's consider the 30 year mortgage for a moment. The power of compound interest is most impressive over long periods of time, like 30 years. Let's say Joe buys the average priced home in America for $215,000 (at the time of this book's writing). Since he is so bad at being patient and saving for the future he finances the whole cost of the house. While these types of loans are harder to find these days, they still exist. In fact, the government encourages them in the form of FHA and VA loans. Basically, the mortgage is designed by the banker for you to pay them money until you are dead (hence the root of the word 'mort'). So let's see how much an average mortgage would cost in America. The payment on this loan will be $1,282.62 at 6 percent interest with nothing down. This doesn't seem too bad does it? It is a lot over 30 years. This is how the salesman gets you to buy very expensive items with "easy, low monthly payments." How much will Joe pay for this average house over the 30 years of bondage? Let's do the easy math together: $1,289.03 X 360 = $464,062!!! Let that sink in for a moment. Joe will pay $249,052 more than the price of the house, for the privilege of living in his average home for 30 years. Not only that, but lenders require debtors to pay mortgage insurance if the debtor does not put 20% of the cost of the home down to protect them from the possibility that the debtor will default on the loan. Mortgage insurance varies, but for an average home it will run somewhere between $100 to $200/month. Think of a 30 year mortgage like throwing $692 dollars a month out the window of your average house. Better yet - think of walking past your local bank EVERY DAY and handing the banker $22.73. This is what a 30 year loan costs. What could you do with $692/month or $22.75/day? You could become very WEALTHI if you used that amount of money to follow the principles of this book.

Some of you proud owners of 30-year death contracts are screaming about the tax write-off that the United States Government has given to people willing to go into debt to buy a house. Joe is an average guy who is in the average marginal tax bracket of 25%. He loves his average house and the tax deduction he gets for his average house. When he starts paying on his new house $1,075 of his $1,289 payment is interest. He gets 25% of this $1,075 or $268.75 that he pays to the bank back from the government as a tax deduction. Now tell me if you think it is a good deal to pay the bank $1,075 in order to get $268.75 back? In more simple terms it is like paying the bank a dollar and getting a quarter back from the government. If you think this is a good idea then make your $1,075 check payable to Darren Smith, and once it clears my checking account, I'll refund you your $268.75. Does this sound like a good idea? Then why do millions of Americans do it? Why did you do it???

The rest of you are probably screaming that there is no way that you can save enough money in your money market account to pay for a house with cash. I admit that in today's society where houses are so expensive, it can be quite difficult to save this amount of money. I can also say that there are people who have done it. However, if you don't want to save for an extended period of time, there is a better way than the 30 year death contract. It is called a 15 year mortgage with a fixed interest rate.

Now consider that Joe reads this book (he is no longer average) and decides that he wants to cut the number of years that he is

40

in bondage to his banker by ½, or 15 years. He also saves for the down payment, so that he doesn't have to pay mortgage insurance and puts down 20%. How long do you think it would take them to save for the $43,000 down payment? If they save their $1290 into a money market account for 32 months, or 2 ¾ years, they will have enough for the down payment. But, you protest, they still have to pay rent while they are saving for the down payment. How can they do that? If they save $792/month for 5 years, they can get to the same $43,000 down payment. I'll explain how they save that much money later. Just know that it involves not having a car payment or credit card payments and cutting back on other expenses. How much more is his mortgage payment? The borrower will also get a quarter point or more discount for a 15 year loan. A $172,000 note at 5.75% interest for 15 years results in a payment of $1428.31 per month or just $139.27 more than the 30 year mortgage. So, by waiting for just 5 years they can have their house paid off 10 years earlier AND be in bondage for 15 fewer years. But it gets better. It also saves them $163,955 over the life of the loan. That does not even count the fact that they didn't actually save all of the $43,000, but some of the down payment came from interest earned at the bank. Let me summarize in the following table.

Loan Type	Cost	Down Payment	Loan Amount	Interest Rate	Monthly Payment	Total Cost
30 Year w/0% Down	$215,000	$0	$215,000	6.00%	$1,289	$464,051
15 Year w/20% Down	$215,000	$43,000	$172,000	5.75%	$1,428	$300,096
				Savings	-$139.28	$163,955

Live Within Your Means

Think of it this way. For the low easy monthly payment of $139.28 you can save $163,955.00 over 15 years. Does this seem like a good plan? Are you beginning to see how being in debt to other people makes you the loser in the game of money? How much better off would you be if you could have $164,000 more in your retirement accounts? Or consider this thought; you could rent out your first house, get a 15 year loan on a second house and own two houses in the time that an average person has paid off their first. The rent from the first house could pay part or all of the mortgage payment on the second. Don't believe this is true? I'll show you how to run the numbers yourself in Appendix B.

When I started my financial education in 2002, I read a book by Robert Kiyosaki. He explained that poor people spend all of their money on expenses. They blow it on rent, beer, cigarettes, rent-to-own appliances, etc. In my mind the poor person needs to get educated so that they can make more money and move up to the middle class. See Chapter 2.

Middle class people have a little more income and therefore typically have more credit. They use the credit to buy cars, houses, boats, motorcycles and all kinds of expensive toys. The middle class also need a financial education. The only way that middle class people can become wealthy is if they start acting like rich people. The rich buy assets and let those assets buy toys for them. They obey the law of the harvest (see Chapter 6) and spend only after they have residual income to pay for the toys.

Regardless of whether you consider yourself poor, middle class or rich, you need to pay off your debts in order to open up cash flow so that you can buy assets. In other words, get out of debt so that you can become rich! Banks can work with you to get wealthy or help you go into bondage. Banks are essentially neutral, kind of like money. They can be used for good or evil. If you go into debt to buy consumer goods, you will be causing financial problems for yourself. If you use banks to save up to buy assets, then you will eliminate problems for yourself.

In life we work for many groups of people. I list a few below, but there are more.

Your employer – Yup, that's right. Your employer takes the first cut of your efforts right off of the top. In order for an employer to take the risk of hiring you they must make more off of your work than they pay you. Sometimes the number is 10 times the salary that they pay you. The only way to avoid this "expense" is to have your own business, and doing so is beyond the scope of this book. There are a myriad of difficulties involved with working for yourself or owning a business where other people work for you. It's not for everyone, but it can pay very well, when done correctly.

God – Not everyone works for God, but some do by paying their tithing. Charitable giving is typically tax deductible, so God takes his cut before the government gets its grubby hands on your money.

The Governments – I use the plural form of government because there are so many in the U.S. There is the Federal, State, City and even Home Owner's Associations (HOAs) that we work for in the form of taxes and fees. I strongly recommend paying your taxes. If you don't, the government may come after you. They could garnish your wages and may even throw you in jail.

The Healthcare Industry - This likely the next largest expense that you have. These expenses have been growing at a rate that is more than double the inflation rate. Part of the reason that they get paid so much is that they extend the lives of the people they care for. It is hard to put a price on this service, but these folks raise the price every year and value their services.

Banks – The next largest expense is probably the interest and fees that we pay to banks. I recommend paying your tithing, your taxes and buying healthcare insurance. Whether or not you start your own business is a question that only you can answer, preferably after some deep study on the subject. I recommend against paying interest and fees to the bank by getting out of debt and keeping a close eye on your finances. When I was starting my financial education, I was a typical middle class person with a car payment and a house payment. I added up the interest that I was paying and it amounted to over $1,000 per month. I was shocked that such a large amount of my money was going to make the bankers rich. I wanted to become wealthy, and not make the banker wealthy. Some people say that we don't change until we become so disgusted with our situation that we are emotionally prompted to act. I was that day. I went out and refinanced my car from a 5 year to a 3 year loan that cut about 1 point off of the interest rate and saved two years of servitude. I also refinanced my house from a 30 year loan at 6 percent to a 15 year loan at 4 5/8 percent. This reduced the amount I paid in interest to banks by a factor of 3. If you have no debt, then congratulations! If you do have debt, then I HIGHLY recommend that you list all of your debts (including your house) and calculate the amount of interest that you are paying to the banks on a monthly basis. You will likely have a similar experience. DO IT NOW! DON'T PROCRASTINATE!!! Get the loans paid off as quickly as you can so that you have money to buy assets! You will have to sacrifice to get it done, but the sacrifice will be worth it. If you follow the plan I outline at the end of this chapter, you will see that you can likely pay off all your debt in 10 to 15 years.

Other Expenses – They include rent, food, transportation, utilities, phone, water and trash, etc. The most common expenses that can be eliminated from this group are the cell phone bill and cable/satellite/internet bill. You don't think you can live without your iPhone and TV service? I'll bet the average person pays more than $150/month on these expenses. How much would $150/month for 40 years at 6% cost a person at retirement? The answer is $298,723.61. I HOPE YOU LIKE TO CHAT WITH YOUR FRIENDS FIND OUT WHO GETS THROWN OFF THE ISLAND because it is costing you dearly! Don't we NEED a cell phone and some kind of digital, high definition entertainment? The answer is no, but I can't argue that these things are not nice. I recommend going cheap for these luxuries. Consider buying a pay as you go phone. I recommend Virgin Mobile, T-Mobile or some other pay-as-you-go cell phone supplier. For $35 to $40 month, you can get unlimited talk and text. I also get 3GB of data in addition to unlimited talk and text with my T-Mobile account for $40/month. They also have plans where they don't charge you monthly fees, but you can "top up" your phone when you want to (or have the money to). They typically charge $0.10 per minute, but they also run sales periodically.

What about entertainment? The cable and satellite companies don't want you to know, but high definition TV is broadcast over the air for free. Get a decent antenna and you can have free programming in high definition. I also recommend buying a Digital Video Recorder (DVR). You can also get these without signing a contract with a cable or satellite provider. I have a DVR that allows me to record over the air content and it works much like a VCR, only better. You can skip commercials with the touch of a button and pause live TV to go to the loo. DVRs cost anywhere from $200 to as much as $1500, but the key is that you pay only once and you can save up to buy them. You have got to get these monthly expenses off of your cash flow statement if you want to become wealthy. It's likely you have a weak spot in one of these areas. You've got to have your cell phone or you can't miss the big game (there's not a lot of sports for free over the air). For me, it's the internet. I have a need for speed, and I can't stand the slow internet providers. There is always the option of going to the library to get free access to the internet. It is OK to splurge in one of these categories, but don't buy phone time you don't use, broadband internet service that goes wasted or TV time that is not watched. In fact, getting rid of one or more of these expenses you will open up time to work harder and learn a new skill (see Chapters 1 and 2).

One of my favorite ways to save money is to completely eliminate your standard telephone service. You know, the "Ma Bell" service that charges extra for long distance. If you have a high speed internet service you can get telephone service over the data lines. It is called Voice Over Internet Protocol (VOIP). There are multiple companies that provide this service which can cut your phone bill by more than half, and domestic long distance is free. I use a service called OOMA that is free. If you want voicemail, call blocking and several other features it costs about $10/month. You have to buy and maintain the hardware, but the monthly expenses are all but eliminated. If you have a cell phone you can completely shut down the service and go without a land line at all.

Here's an example of how you can reduce your expenses by $200.

Monthly Expense	Cell Phone	Cable TV	High Speed Internet	Land Line Telephone vs. VOIP	Totals
Current Expenses	$100	100	50	50	$300
New Reduced Expenses	$40	0	50	10	$100
*Over the air HD TV substituted for HD Cable and VOIP substituted for traditional phone line	-$60	$100	-$0	-$40	-$200

So how is getting out of debt to be accomplished? Here is the simple, yet difficult, plan to follow.

Debt Elimination Plan

1) Reduce your expenses by at least $100 - 200 per month (see previous table).
2) Apply that extra money to your smallest debt and make minimum payments on all other debts.
3) When the smallest debt is paid off, wrap your extra money, plus the payment for your smallest debt into the second smallest debt.
4) Repeat step 3 until all of your debt is paid off.
5) Once your debt is paid off then use your now significant cash flow to buy assets (see Chapter 7, "Insurance and Investing" for the types of assets that I recommend).

It is up to you whether or not to include your house in this process that I call the debt elimination plan. You will likely have on the order of $500 - $800 cash flow opened up when you have paid off everything except your house. If you wrap your house into the debt elimination plan you could have $1500 or $2000/month cash flow. Can you envision what you could do with $2,000 more cash flow? It is possible if you pay off your house! Your house likely has a low interest rate, and the interest paid is tax deductible. If you don't pay off your house with the debt elimination plan then refinance to a 15 year loan if you don't already have one and you have more than 15 years left on your loan.

It is really a simple process that anyone with debt can follow. However, it is not easy. It takes sacrifice and patience. Both of these qualities are rare in America, and I'm willing to bet most of the world. Ten to fifteen years is a LONG time, but it sure beats working for the banker the rest of your life!

Some of you may say that it would be faster to pay off the debt with the highest interest rate first, and if you have the discipline to do it that way, then you would be right. However, most people need to see some results early on in the debt elimination plan. Seeing that credit card bill go down in flames gives you the motivation to move on to the next largest bill. Personal finance is more about psychology than it is about math (although the math is important too). It is likely that the time required to pay off your debts, smallest to largest, is only months longer and not years longer than paying it off with the highest interest first, even if you include your house. If you get discouraged because it takes too long to pay off your highest interest loan first and give up on the debt elimination plan, it will cost you a whole lot more money than a few months of interest. If you don't believe me, run the numbers on a spreadsheet. If you are not spreadsheet savvy, then I recommend getting a financial calculator. See Appendix B for directions on how to use a financial calculator and a spreadsheet to determine how long it will take to pay off your debts. I also recommend Dave Ramsey's book, *The Total Money Makeover* as a good way to get motivated to get out of debt.

EXAMPLE: Peter NotsoPerfect and MollyMakesMistakes save $200/month, following the advice in this chapter and want to get out of debt with the debt elimination plan. Here is their fictitious story:

Debt	Balance	Interest	Minimum Payment	Actual Payment	Pay Off Time
Discover	$250	15%	$10	$210	2 Months
Visa	$750	12%	$15	$225	+3 Months
AMEX	$1,000	18%	$20	$245	+4 Months
Furniture	$6,500	10%	$130	$375	+17 Months
Car(s)	$10,000	8%	$210	$585	+11 Months
House	$65,000	6%	$701	$1,286	+44 Months

In less than 7 years, they have all of their debt retired and can start acquiring assets to make themselves wealthy. Keep reading to see how.

Chapter 5 – Tithing and Time Value of Money

Tithing

The "T" in WEALTHI stands for Tithing and the Time value of money. Why would I bring up the topic of tithing in a non-religious book? Even if you don't believe in God or Karma or you have no religious beliefs at all, there is a law of the universe that is stated simply, "You get from the universe what you give to the universe." If you want to become wealthy, you should help others build wealth. If you want assistance starting a small business, you should help others start a small business. If you want help to find a job, you should help others find a job. I like the way that Suzie Orman puts it. Loosely paraphrased, Ms. Orman writes, In order to receive you have to open your hand to give. Just about every competent investment specialist recommends giving in order to become wealthy.

I define tithing as giving 10 percent of your gross income to charity. The law of tithing is contrary to what you might think you should do in order to obtain wealth. Shouldn't you hoard all of your money and invest it to the best of your ability? The answer, it turns out, is NO. When you give to others, you learn to live on less than you make. Living beneath your means (Chapter 4, "Live Within Your Means") is the most critical discipline to learn in order to become wealthy. When you give money to charitable organizations or to other people you must live beneath your means to pay all of your expenses. It then becomes even easier to live farther below your means to save and invest money. However, paying tithing also unlocks Divine Providence in your favor.

Tithing and Time Value Of Money

Let me give you an example. I have paid tithing to my church my entire life. When I was laid off in 2002 after the horrific 9/11 attack on my country, I had an experience that I can only be explained by Divine Providence. When I was laid off, my company gave me the equivalent of 5 months of severance pay after only 5 years of service. They also sent me to a job search class that taught me valuable resume writing, interviewing and networking skills. However, these blessings are only part of the providence I speak of. One day, when I had been out of work for more than a month, I walked into church and got a strong impression that I should talk to a young man who had recently started attending the congregation. Not really knowing why, I sat down and introduced myself. The conversation eventually got around to the fact that I was looking for work. He told me how his father-in-law was looking for someone to do mechanical design. The young man gave me his father-in-law's contact information and I had a job within a week.

While 2002 was quite stressful for me and my family, it was also the best year of my life because I had a significant emotional experience that started me on my path to gaining a financial education. It wasn't fun, but it was a great learning experience.

The way that I look at tithing is this: I want to have God on my side in my quest to become wealthy. One of the few good things you can do with money is to give it to other people. Money gives a person power, and a wealthy person has the power to help other people. If you show God that you are willing to help others on your path to become wealthy, you will be more likely to help others when you become VERY WEALTHY. You will become very wealthy if you follow the guidelines outlined in this book. God will be more likely to help you get gain if you impart some of it to his other children.

But you might be saying that 10 percent is a lot. You would be surprised at how easy it is to give 10 percent. If you absolutely can't see giving 10 percent, then give one percent. If you are not religious, then give to your favorite charity. I am certain you have something or some organization that you believe in or support. Congratulations if you are already giving 10 percent. You probably know the blessings that come by doing so. If you are not, then I suggest this plan. Whenever you get a raise, take half of that raise and save it for your future. Take the other half and increase your charitable giving. You will be greatly blessed if you learn to live beneath your means and learn to give to others. I leave you with one last thought that I believe to be true in more than financial matters. Malachi 3:10 reads, "Bring ye all the tithes into the storehouse, that there may be meat in mine house, and prove me now herewith, saith the LORD of hosts, if I will not open you the windows of heaven, and pour you out a blessing, that *there shall not be room enough to receive it.*" Italics added for emphasis.

The Time Value of Money

Now that you have a reason to become wealthy, make a little more from working hard and getting training, tracking your expenses, and living beneath your means, you will have a little money to invest. What can you do with this money? Chapter 7, "Insurance and Investing," describes in detail my investment recommendations. However, I'll give you a little preview here. I recommend investing the largest part of your investment money in equities. Equity is stock in a business venture, whether it is your own company, a private venture or the public stock market. Since most people don't have their own business and are not wealthy enough to invest in private firms, I will focus on public stocks.

For the last 130 years, public stocks have returned between 9 and 11 percent. Taking inflation into account, this translates into 6 to 8 percent real return on your money. Most financial advisors like to use a 10 percent return when speaking of investing in the stock market. I like to be more realistic, especially considering the fact that the stock market has had periods as long as 20 years when it has returned nothing in terms of capital gains. Even when there are no capital gains or increases in the underlying value of stock investment, you get dividends that currently average about 2 percent. Let's look at what a 7% return can get you over time.

What if you were to invest your new car payment of $500/month for 10, 20, 30 or even 40 years and get a 7% return on your money? The time value of money is an amazing thing, as you have already noticed in the example I gave about the 30-year mortgage. It is even more amazing when it works in your favor. I show an example here of investing $500 dollars a month using conservative, moderate and aggressive strategies. Assuming 3 percent, 5 percent and 6 percent returns for these strategies the following results are expected ON AVERAGE. I recommend that you keep at least some of your money invested in bonds or some other fixed income security. The reason for this is the fact that bonds are negatively correlated to stocks. In other words, when stocks go down, bonds tend to go up. This allows you to rebalance periodically and buy low and sell high. More on the concept of buy low and sell high later. Having some bonds also helps dampen the bumpy ride of the stock market. Too many ups and downs can cause normally rational people to behave irrationally and do stupid things with their money – like selling all of their stocks when the market crashes. I made this mistake when I first started investing in the stock market.

Note that the following numbers are just an estimate and not guarantees of future results. These numbers also include an estimated 3% inflation.

Monthly Payment	$503			
Investor Type	Term (Years)/ Interest Rate	10	20	30	40
Paranoid (100% Bonds)	2%	$66,758	$148,283	$247,841	$369,421
Conservative (20% Stocks)	3%	$70,290	$165,136	$293,117	$465,808
Moderate (60% Stocks)	5%	$78,107	$206,750	$418,626	$767,588
Aggressive (80% Stocks)	6%	$82,431	$232,407	$505,271	$1,001,720
All In (100% Stocks)	7%	$87,062	$262,026	$613,645	$1,320,281

This estimate assumes compound interest on your investment and the stock market. So, if you sacrifice the new car and drive used cars for 40 years, you could be a millionaire. This is a simple strategy that anyone can apply to be very wealthy. Albert Einstein has been quoted as saying that the greatest marvel of the universe is that of compound interest. These may or may not be Einstein's words, but if you save $503/month in an 80% stock portfolio you could be a millionaire in 40 years. If you give up that $500/month and buy or lease new cars your whole life you will look really cool, but you won't be wealthy. Stanley and Denko in the *Millionaire Next Door* mention that in

Texas this is called, "Big Hat, No Cattle." In Colorado this might be termed, "Big Reel, No Fish."

The numbers aren't as good if you have less time to invest. The more time you have the more value your money will accrue. However, if you are getting on in years and have procrastinated your investing, all is not lost. You probably make more money if you are older and therefore can invest more money. What if you could save $3,000/month? It is possible if you are completely out of debt, the kids are out on their own (if you have any) and you are into your high income earning years.

Monthly Payment	$3,000		
Investor Type	Term (Years)/ Interest Rate	10	20
Paranoid (100% Bonds)	2%	$398,159	$884,391
Conservative (20% Stocks)	3%	$419,224	$984,906
Moderate (60% Stocks)	5%	$465,847	$1,233,101
Aggressive (80% Stocks)	6%	$491,638	$1,386,123
All In (100% Stocks)	7%	$519,254	$1,562,780

If you were able to save $3000/month for just 10 years, you could have about half a million dollars by investing aggressively. If you only have 10 years until retirement, you are also more likely to get Social Security benefits and have a pension. If you can't come up with such a large monthly sum to invest, you can consider putting off retirement for another 5 years. You will end up with more money, and have less time that you will need to use that money.

So what if your situation doesn't fall into one of the above tables that I have included here? The calculations are fairly simple and I have included instructions on how to run them on a financial calculator and spreadsheet in Appendix B. It is extremely fast to use a spreadsheet or a financial calculator that you can pick up for $20 or $30. If you have Microsoft Excel or even Microsoft Works, you can also do these calculations fairly quickly and create your own tables.

Chapter 6 – Harvesting Your Efforts

The Law of the Harvest

The "H" in WEALTHI stands for Harvest in the WEALTHI acronym. Think about a farmer for a moment. There is no way to short cut the law of the harvest if you are a farmer. The ground must be prepared by adding the proper nutrients and turning over the soil. Given the climate and the soil, the right kind of seed needs to be planted. An irrigation system, preferably an automatic irrigation system, has to be set up to water the seeds. Weeds must be pulled or sprayed periodically to prevent the unwanted plants from strangling the crops. If all this work is done diligently, the crops will be ready to harvest. A sacrifice must be made before the harvest comes. Even when you do all that you can, an early hail or snowstorm may still destroy the crop. To be successful, the farmer has to be diligent over the years and never give up.

Becoming wealthy is a lot like being a farmer. The ground is your personal finances. They must be prepared by creating a budget and eliminating debt. The unnecessary expenses must be plucked out like weeds so that there is room for the seed money to grow. You must set up a monthly investment plan in order to water your investments. Just like the irrigation system, it is best to have an automatic system set up that invests on a monthly basis. You need to invest in the right kind of investments given the kind of climate where you live. All of these things must be done over time so that you can harvest your crop of wealth when needed. Even if you have prepared, sacrificed and saved, there may be a market crash or a job layoff that sets you back for a year or so. You need to be consistent, year after year, and pay your tithing so that Divine Providence is on your side when the hail comes.

I am waxing a bit philosophical here, but you need to understand that while living beneath your means may be the most important thing you do to become wealthy, you must do it consistently and over time. The analogy of the diet works here. A diet might help you lose weight in the short run, but if you don't make lifestyle changes, the weight will come back. The WEALTHI plan is not a quick fix or get rich quick plan, but it is a plan to build wealth over time and have that wealth last. It is not how much money you make, but how much you keep and how you invest it that matters.

How do you build up the discipline to sacrifice for long periods of time? It all starts with the 'Why' from Chapter 1. If you don't keep the goal in mind then you will not have the fortitude to persevere. Stephen Coveys book, *The 7 Habits of Highly Effective People* talks about keeping the end in mind. While his book takes a more holistic view of your entire life, it can be applied to wealth building. How do you see yourself when you become wealthy? Are you travelling the world without having to worry about the cost of doing so? Are you living in your dream house with time to spend with your family? Do you get to spend time working at your life's calling, rather than just a job? You've got to find your 'Why' to develop the fortitude to sacrifice to get there. I also like Dave Ramsey's saying, "You've got to live like no one else, so that later, you can live like no one else."

What does it take to get to the point where you have what you want and are who you want to be? It takes clearly written goals and a plan to achieve those goals. If you have not done so yet, get a piece of paper and write down what your goals are and why you want to achieve them. Don't just type them into a computer, but put pen to paper and physically write them down or print them out. If you have not already learned, paper lasts a whole lot longer than any type of electronic media. You may even want to laminate your goals. Once you have done so then list each goal on a separate piece of paper and write down the specific sacrifices you are going to make in order to reach each goal. Remember that to sacrifice means to give away something good in return for something better.

Honesty

The "H" in WEALTHI also stands for Honesty. Tom Stanley also wrote a book called *The Millionaire Mind*. He embarked on researching what it takes to become a deca-millionaire. He did extensive research on individuals who amassed tens of millions of dollars. One of the traits that these deca-millionaires had was integrity. They could be trusted to do what they said they would do. These people met their customer or employer demands and delivered their products or projects on time and on schedule. When a person can be trusted to get the job done, they typically are rewarded with additional jobs. My current employer calls this the do/say ratio. You need to approach 100% of what you do matching what you say you will do.

Let me give an example of the opposite type of person. I have four old, used cars that often need oil changes. There was (emphasis on *was*) a service station near my home that offered a coupon that allowed the holder to get an oil change for free if he paid for ten oil changes in a given period of time. My wife and I purchased the ten oil changes in the allotted amount of time, with about a month to spare. When we presented the coupon and proof of purchase for the 10 oil changes, we were denied the eleventh free oil change. We clearly explained the situation and showed the evidence of our purchase to the owner of the service station. He still refused the free oil change. He had no intention of honoring his coupon. I threatened to take my business elsewhere to which he responded, "What business?!?!" My wife and I became irate and never went back to the service station. It would likely have cost him ten or fifteen dollars to honor his coupon and we may have come back for our other service needs. Four cars that are ten-plus years old need a lot of maintenance. It was not long before he was out of business and a new owner moved into the location. I'm not trying to imply that my wife and I caused his business to fail. I am saying that his business likely failed if he treated all of his customers in this fashion.

The bottom line is that it pays to be honest. If you are trustworthy, people will pay you to solve their problems. Honesty is a simple concept that if followed, will reap a great harvest.

Chapter 7 – Insurance and Investing

Insurance

In my mind, insurance is a necessary evil. Why do I say that it is evil? The problem with insurance is that, on average, you are guaranteed to lose. The insurance company has to make a profit for its investors and at the same time cover all of its costs, including the payment of claims, sales, marketing, employee salaries, office overhead, etc. As a whole, people who buy insurance policies are guaranteed to pay out more than they take in, making insurance a net loss proposition. It's kind of like a morbid lottery. In a lottery, you pay a little money with the hope you will beat the odds and get a big sum of money. With insurance you are betting against the odds that you will have a problem, and if you do the insurance company will help out with some money. I do not recommend spending money on the lottery, but I do recommend investing in insurance.

Why do I say that insurance is necessary? The fact of the matter is that when you build up some assets you need to have insurance to protect those assets. We all have assets. Even if the only asset you have is your health, you need to protect it. Insurance is necessary, especially in our litigious society, to protect you against catastrophic loss. What if you were to die or become severely disabled? How would your loved ones get by? What if you get into a car accident and either get injured or injure someone else? How would you pay your medical bills or those of the person(s) you injured? Insurance is necessary. You don't want all the hard work you have done to become wealthy, only to have that wealth disappear due to a catastrophic event.

So what kind of insurance do you need? I am not an expert on insurance for the reasons I have already listed. However, I do know that you need health insurance, life insurance if people depend on your income, disability insurance, auto insurance, home owners insurance if you own a home or renter's insurance if you rent, and long term care insurance if you are 60 years of age or older.

Health Insurance

The number one cause of bankruptcy is unpaid medical bills. Hospitals are required to give you emergency medical assistance if you need it, and if you survive they will send you a bill. If you do not have insurance, you will be required to pay the entire balance. If you cannot pay or cannot get a loan to pay the bill they will send a collection agency after you and may sue to get every penny they can. As a result, a lot of people file for bankruptcy. I am not demeaning the medical industry. It is filled with highly skilled people who provide services that we all need sooner or later. They deserve to be paid and we all need to figure out how to pay for their services. For most of us, that means buying health insurance. If you do not have an employer who pays most of the cost of the insurance, I recommend getting a high deductible insurance policy because the monthly/yearly premiums are lower. You can budget for yearly annual expenses and use your emergency fund to pay for deductibles in the event of a major medical problem. In the United States, you can open a Health Savings Account (HSA) if you have a high deductible insurance policy. An HSA allows you to save money, tax free, to pay for medical expenses. It is like a traditional IRA that you can pull money out of, tax free, to cover your medical expenses. I have one of these with a debit card that allows me to automatically pull money out for medical expenses. I can also use the online bill payment service to pay for expenses with a check. The nice thing about these accounts is that they act like a retirement account if you don't need the money for medical expenses. You can take the money out, penalty free, once you are 65 years old. You will have to pay taxes if you don't use the money for medical expenses, just like a traditional IRA. The current yearly limits for HSAs are $3,350 for individuals and $6,750 for families. I recommend saving the maximum amount allowed by the IRS into your HSA account.

Life Insurance

If you have loved ones who depend on your income, you need life insurance. What would happen to your spouse or children if you died suddenly? Would they be able to cover their expenses, or would they have to significantly downsize their lifestyle just to get by? Would they even be able to pay for your burial expenses? I recommend term life insurance because it is significantly less expensive than the other types of insurance. The "term" means that the insurance is only good for a limited amount of time. Why would you want insurance that expires? If you are on the path to becoming wealthy then you will be able to self-insure. The "term" also means that your payment will stay the same over the term of your insurance policy. After 20 or 30 years you should be wealthy enough to self-insure. In other words, your assets should be able to take care of your loved ones if you die unexpectedly. If they are not disabled or have other health issues, your children should also be able to take care of themselves by the time the insurance policy ends.

Long-Term Disability Insurance

For similar reasons, you need to get long-term disability insurance. If you were disabled and could not work anymore, how would your loved ones pay for your expenses? It's also likely that your medical expenses will increase significantly if you become severely disabled. I recommend getting disability insurance that will cover at least 50 percent of your current income should you become permanently disabled. There is likely some social safety net where you live, such as Social Security in the United States, that will help offset some of the loss of income. You need to have some way to support yourself and your family if you become disabled.

Auto Insurance

Auto insurance is required by law in the United States. For this reason alone, you should get auto insurance. If you have an accident or get a traffic violation and don't have insurance, you could lose your license or be thrown into jail. You should have liability auto insurance in the event that you have an accident and it turns out to be your fault. You need to be able to pay the expenses of other people that you hurt if you are at fault and/or get sued for damages. You will also have to pay for any damages that you incur to other people's vehicles. Don't let an accident wipe you out financially. If you cannot afford to replace your car with your emergency fund then you should also get comprehensive auto insurance. However, if this is the case, you likely have a car that you cannot afford. Consider selling the car, buying a less expensive used car and saving the difference for an emergency fund.

Home Owner's and Renter's Insurance

Home owner's and renter's insurance are necessary to protect your home and belongings in case of fire, theft or some other emergency. A recent fire near my home made me glad that I have insurance on my home. While I would not like to lose my home, it is nice to know that I could replace it and my belongings if the fire had reached my home.

Long-Term Care Insurance

If you are 60 or older, you need long-term care insurance. Long-term care insurance will help pay for the cost of nursing home care or home help, if needed. If you are younger than 60 years of age then you have less than a 1 percent chance of needing long term care, and your disability insurance will cover you in the event that you become dependent on others. In the event that you become mentally or physically unable to take care of yourself, you will need help. A decent nursing home will cost more than $40,000/year per person. If this happens you will likely have higher medical expenses than you would if you were living without assistance.

Investing

What is a person to do when he has worked hard, gotten an education and/or professional training, tracked his expenses, lived beneath his means, purchased insurance and stayed the course to the point where he has some cash flow to invest? You can make investing as easy or as difficult as you want to. There are reams of financial data that are generated every day and hundreds of pundits who comment on the data. I submit that it is not necessary to go over all of this data and make it your personal hobby. In fact, a simple investment plan is the best.

I have outlined several steps for you to follow below, and I will expand on each step later on in this chapter.

Step 1) Invest enough in your 401k to get your employer match.

Step 2) Pay off your consumer debt.

Step 3) Build an emergency fund of 6 months of your expenses.

Step 4) Buy real estate for your personal residence.

Step 5) Buy equities, otherwise known as stock in businesses.

Step 6) Diversify your investments.

Step 7) Quit your day job, if you want to.

Step 1) Invest enough in your 401k to get your employer match!

Not all people have a 401k or even an employer for that matter. However, if you do, then you need to take advantage of the incredible benefit of the employer match your company is offering. Many employers are doing away with their defined benefit pension plans in exchange for the 401k plans that are named after a section of the IRS tax code. This change basically shifts the risk from the employer to the employee. Previously, the employer was responsible for investing money so they would have assets that would provide income for their employees at retirement. Now they are shifting that burden to employees. Employers often offer to match employee contributions to a 401k plan. This match can be anywhere from 25 percent of what the employee puts in up to two times the amount the employee puts in. Typically this number is a 50 percent match, so I will limit my examples to a 50 percent match. On average, for every dollar that an employee contributes, the employer provides 50 cents.

Some of you are screaming that you should get out of debt or save for an emergency before contributing to a 401k plan. You might have an argument if your employer matches 25 percent or less, and I would definitely agree if your employer doesn't match at all. The reason I think you should start by investing in the 401k if your employer matches 50 percent or more is that you simply cannot get an instant 50 percent passive return on your money anywhere else. At the writing of this book, the worst credit cards charge interest rates in the 30 percent range. My home state of Colorado has a limit of 42 percent that creditors can charge. The exception to this rule is the payday lender or the consignment/rent to own places that charge ridiculous interest rates up to 700 percent. If you have any of these types of loans, pay them off as fast as you can and avoid them in the future.

So what about the emergency fund? Shouldn't you build up an emergency fund before you put money in your 401k? My answer is a resounding NO. If your employer matches at least 50 percent of the money you put into a 401k you should use your 401k as your emergency fund. I can hear the screams from the financial planners out there saying that if you withdraw money from your 401k that you will have to pay a 10 percent penalty if you are younger than 59 ½ and pay income taxes. I say that the 10 percent penalty and the taxes are less than the 50 percent match you would be missing out on, so you've got to get that match! Some leading financial planners say that you will pay 40 percent in order to get money out of your 401k, and that may be true in some instances, but 40 percent is still less than a 50 percent match and I'll prove it! In fact, you come out ahead by putting your money in the 401k and getting the 50 percent match up to the point where your tax bracket is 70 percent. We haven't seen such a high tax bracket since Jimmy Carter was president. It is unlikely, though possible, that we will see income taxes that high in the future. Until then, my advice holds true.

Here's an example to prove my point. Say you make an average income and you are in the marginal tax bracket of 25 percent. You would have to pay a 10 percent penalty and 25 percent taxes on the money you would take out of a 401k plan. Note, however, that if you were saving your money into a traditional money market account, you would pay taxes on your money BEFORE it got into the money market account. Here's a matrix to show the difference between the traditional method and the way I suggest you save for emergencies.

Emergency Fund Savings Vehicle	Savings	Tax Rate	Initial Taxes	Employer Match	Total Saved	Penalty	Taxes	Emergency Savings
50 percent Employer Matched 401k Plan	$10,000	25%	$0	$5,000	$15,000	$1,500	$3,750	$9,750
Traditional Money Market Account	$10,000	25%	$2,500	$0	$7,500	$0	$0	$7,500
							Benefit	$2,250

In a similar fashion, you can see how the benefit decreases as your marginal tax rate increases to the point where there is no benefit upon withdrawal at a 70 percent marginal tax rate.

Marginal Tax Rate	Savings Amount	401k Withdrawal	Money Market	Difference
10.0 percent	$10,000	$12,000	$9,000	$3,000
15.0 percent	$10,000	$11,250	$8,500	$2,750
25.0 percent	$10,000	$9,750	$7,500	$2,250
33.0 percent	$10,000	$8,550	$6,700	$1,850
35.0 percent	$10,000	$8,250	$6,500	$1,750
39.6 percent	$10,000	$7,560	$6,040	$1,520
70.0 percent	$10,000	$3,000	$3,000	$0

Even if your marginal tax rate were 70 percent, I would argue that it is better to invest in the 401k with a match because you may not have to withdraw the money. Not everyone has emergencies, and if you can plow through to step 3 before you have an emergency, you will have your company's match working for you your whole life. It would be better to invest enough in your 401k to get the employer match AND have a cash emergency fund, but when your lack of disposable income forces you to choose, I recommend the 401k in order to get the match.

What if you don't have an employer match? The answer is you must save a little for emergencies. I recommend 2 percent of your gross income. If your household has an income of $75,000/year then you should save approximately $1,500 for emergencies. This will cover the small emergencies that come into your life, such as the shingles getting blown off of your roof, or the dishwasher going out or minor car repairs. All of these things happened to me in the last year. You need to have a little bit saved for these things, even before you embark on paying off your consumer debt.

Step 2) Pay off consumer debt

If you have made it this far into the book it should be evident that paying off your consumer debt is important. You will open up cash flow that you can use to become wealthy by doing so. If you have credit card bills, car loans, personal loans or loans for expensive toys then pay them off. Pay off everything that is not associated with real estate or some income producing investment. The average interest rate on credit cards is 14 percent. This interest rate is higher than you can expect to earn in good investments that I will recommend. Pay off your credit cards and pay them off now! Personal loans for consumer products, including automobiles, also charge interest rates high enough that they need to be paid off. Use the Debt Elimination Plan, as described in Chapter 4, "Live Within Your Means," to pay off all of your debt with the exception of your primary residence.

3) Build an Emergency Fund

Build an emergency fund of 6 months of your expenses in addition to your 401k. If you do not know what your expenses are then go back to chapters 3 and 4 and build a cash flow statement. This money should be held in a liquid account where you can get to it quickly. This money should be used for emergencies like paying the deductible on your medical insurance policy or buying food to eat if you get laid off from your job. It is not for "emergencies" like Christmas. Christmas comes at the same time every year and can be accounted for in a budget. It is also not for "emergencies" like a sale at the local department store. Merchants have sales all the time, and if you have budgeted for clothing you can take advantage of them with the cash you have budgeted for clothing. This fund is like your umbrella in the event that it will rain. You will have emergencies, so you need to prepare for them. Six months of savings will cover the typical expenses incurred by a layoff. If you have not gotten a new equivalent or better source of income within 6 months, then you will likely have to look at downgrading your lifestyle.

4) Buy real estate for your personal residence.

Buy an apartment, condo or house for your personal residence. Save enough money to put at least 20 percent down or pay cash. Get a fixed 15 year loan if you do not put 100 percent down. If owning real estate is not for you, move on to step 5. Real estate can be a great long term investment because it provides a forced savings vehicle. This is especially true about your primary residence because you have to live somewhere. Just keep in mind that owning a house costs more than renting, in the beginning, due to the maintenance costs.

Why buy a house if renting is cheaper? The answer lies in the fact that if you buy a house you can fix this expense or at least part of the expense forever. Rent goes up with inflation. Every year your landlord will likely raise your rent. If you get a fixed-rate mortgage, your payment will stay the same over the life of the loan, and once the loan is paid off, the mortgage expense goes away entirely! You will still have maintenance expenses and taxes to pay, but these will be much cheaper than renting, and you will have money to invest to become wealthy. It turns out that 15-year loans pay off in 15 years, and that 15 years goes by much faster than you would expect. I just paid off my primary residence, and as a result, have opened up significant cash flow to help me become wealthy.

If you do not have a 20 percent down payment, rent an inexpensive place and save money until you have enough for a down payment. If you do not have a 20 percent down payment in cash, then I submit that you are too broke to buy a house. If you don't have the discipline to save for the down payment, then you likely don't have the discipline to own a house. This may sound harsh, but there is a reason that lending institutions require you to have Private Mortgage Insurance (PMI) if you don't have a 20 percent down payment. This insurance is not for you; it is for the bank in the event that you default on your mortgage. It ensures that the bank will get paid what it is owed. If you put 20 percent down, you have a buffer in the event that your house goes down in value. You will still be able to sell your house if it goes down in value by 20 percent. If your house goes down in value, and you have made a zero or small down payment, then you will have to bring a check to the closing table in order to sell the house! If you don't have that money (and you likely won't as you didn't use it for the down payment in the first place), you won't be able to sell your house without special permission from the bank. Putting 20 percent down also shows that you are responsible enough to save your money for a large purchase. Do not use your emergency fund for your down payment! When you buy a house, you open up a whole new category of emergencies. If you are renting, the landlord pays for things like broken toilets, leaky roofs and appliances that die. If you own your house, then you need an emergency fund. Save up a 20 percent down payment in addition to your emergency fund. In fact, you may need to increase your emergency fund due to the additional expenses of home maintenance and home owner's insurance.

How much of a house should you buy? *The Millionaire Next Door* provides an example in which the authors told a young man to hold a mortgage note on his house not greater than 2 times his annual income. If you have a household income of $75,000, you should get a mortgage less than or equal to $150,000. A mortgage payment on a 15 year loan with a 6 percent interest rate on a $150,000 loan would be roughly $1,250. Interest rates are currently much lower than 6 percent, but I don't believe they will stay so low for long. Another way to think about this is the payment on the note should not be more than 25 percent of borrowers' gross income. Some of you may be thinking that you could not buy much house for $150,000. Remember that this number does not include the down payment. With a 20 percent down payment the house would be worth $187,500. This amount of money would buy a modest house in most areas of the United States. If you desire to have a bigger or nicer house, then save up a larger down payment. Remember that 100 percent of the homes in foreclosure have a mortgage on them. I recently read that 10 percent of home owners with mortgages are behind on their payments. Don't become one of these people. Make sure that you own the house, and that the house does not own you!

Banks will loan you more than two times your gross income for a house. Don't be sweet talked into doing so by a realtor or a mortgage broker. They make a larger commission when you buy more house. The larger the debt the greater the risk that you won't be able to pay it off. Some of you may think that this advice is extreme or too much of a sacrifice. I'm telling you that you need to sacrifice in order to become wealthy. Buy a modest home now and pay it off in 15 years or fewer, and you will be able to save enough money to buy your dream house with cash! Keep reading to find out how.

If home ownership is not for you, then I recommend putting some of your money into a Real Estate Investment Trust (REIT). These are securities (see the next section) that allow you to hold part ownership in companies that invest in real estate. These accounts are required by the government to return a certain percentage of the income they generate to you. I recommend holding them in a tax advantaged accounts, such as an IRA or 401k due to the income that they generate.

5) Buy equities, otherwise known as stock.

Equities are ownership in a business venture. The business could be your own business, a private business or a public company. Buy as much stock in companies as you can tolerate from a risk standpoint as stocks have outperformed every other asset class throughout history. If you are in your 20s, I recommend investing at least 10 percent of your income into stocks. If you are in your 30s and have not started saving for retirement, invest 15 percent of your income into equities. Similarly, if you are in your 40s and have not started saving then invest 20 percent in equities. If you are 50 or older and have not started saving, then invest as much of your disposable income as you can stand. Even in your 50s you have plenty of time to save. With average life expectancies hovering around 80 years of age, 50 is still relatively young. Not only are you still young, but you likely make more money than you ever have in your lifetime and can afford to sock away big chunks of money. To become wealthy, I cannot stress the importance of investing over time in equities.

Before I discuss what to invest in, I will describe what kinds of investment vehicles to put your equities into. As previously described, taxes are a huge drain on your income. You should take advantage of every tax-advantaged investment vehicle that you can afford to use. There are two basic types of tax-advantaged retirement accounts in the United States; tax deferred and non-tax deferred. The most common are the traditional Individual Retirement Account (IRA), Health Savings Account (HSA) and 401k. These are accounts that you may put your money into tax deferred. Many financial books and advisors claim that this money is tax free. It is not tax free, but tax deferred. Uncle Sam will get your tax money. You just need to decide whether it will be sooner or later. Tax deferred means that the government will get your tax money when you take it out of the account. If you take money out of a traditional IRA or

401k before you are 59 ½ years of age, you will also pay a 10 percent penalty on the amount withdrawn to the government in addition to taxes that you owe on the entire amount that you withdraw. The benefit of a traditional retirement account is that you get to reduce your taxable income for the current year by the amount you put in. If you are in a high marginal tax bracket with few tax credits and deductions, this may be the primary place to invest your money. As previously mentioned, the HSA is a special kind of tax deferred account that allows you to use money taken out of the account for healthcare without incurring penalties or taxes. I recommend maxing out the HSA due to the fact that healthcare expenses are increasing much faster than inflation. If you take the money out before you are 65 years old and don't use it for healthcare expenses, you will incur the 10 percent penalty in addition to paying taxes on the money. Find an HSA that allows you to invest in equities. Invest enough in your HSA to cover your health insurance deductibles in a money market account and invest the remainder in equities.

The second type of retirement account is called Roth after Senator Roth who wrote the bill to create these types of accounts. Roth accounts allow the investor to put money in after taxes have been paid. All gains from the investments are tax free. I am very fond of Roth IRAs and Roth 401ks for several reasons. You have more control over your money when you invest it in a Roth. You can take out what you have put in (not the gains) without penalty and taxes because you have already paid taxes on the principal. If you have an emergency, the money can be pulled out to pay expenses. If you pull the gains out before you are 59 ½, you will pay the 10 percent penalty and taxes on the money. The other nice thing about Roth accounts is that you don't ever have to take the money out. You must begin taking money out of a traditional 401k by the time you are 70 ½ years old or the government imposes a 50 percent penalty on the amount that the government required you to take out. Basically, Uncle Sam is saying, "I have waited 70 years to get my taxes, and you better give them to me now!" Roth accounts can be held until you die and then passed on to your beneficiaries tax free! You should max out your Roth IRA and Roth 401k account if you can, especially if you are in a low marginal tax bracket with lots of tax credits and deductions. Income taxes are very low relative to historical rates. A huge national debt and even larger federal liabilities lead me to believe that taxes will go up in the future, so it might be a good idea to pay taxes now and invest your money in Roth accounts. There are income limits for the tax benefits of IRAs, but not 401ks. Contact a professional tax advisor to find out if a traditional or Roth (or a combination of both) is right for you. Both types are worth looking into.

So, what should you invest in? What types of stock should you buy? Let me first give you my three rules of investing. If you use these three rules, you should be able to retire with dignity.

Rule #1) Diversify your investments.

Rule #2) Minimize your expenses.

Rule #3) Buy low and sell high.

These rules have been repeated so many times that they may sound trite or even cliché. The reason that they are so familiar is that they work! If done correctly they will ensure that you do not waste your 10 percent, 15 percent, 20 percent or more that you have saved for retirement.

You may be thinking to yourself, "What about the first 10 years of the 21st Century? Wouldn't we have lost money if we had invested this way?" The answer is a resounding NO! I invested with these three rules during the "aughts" (2000 – 2009) and became wealthy.

Rule #1) Diversify your investments.

Investing in the stock of a company is a risky affair. The stocks of companies go up and they go down. Sometimes stocks go completely out of business. Why should you risk your hard earned money in such a risky affair? The answer is that equities provide the best long term investment you can buy. The stock broker, otherwise known as a stock salesperson, will tell you that stocks have gone up on average 10 percent per year throughout recorded history. This is not a lie, but is not the whole truth. The Standard and Poor's 500 Index has gone up nearly 10 percent on average over its recorded history. The S&P 500 is a list of the 500 largest stocks on the American stock exchanges. Smaller public stocks, called small cap stocks, have gone up about 11 percent over recorded history. However, what the stock salesman does not tell you is that stocks don't go up in a straight line. They go up in a choppy random manner that averages out to 10 percent per year over long periods of time. This 10 percent also includes inflation that has averaged out to be about 3 percent over the last 200 years, so the real return is about 7 percent. Still, 7 percent or 8 percent is better than most other passive investments (an investment that you don't have to work at), so you should have some of your money in stocks.

Consider the example of a 5 year old boy skipping down the road to the market with a basket full of 30 eggs. What happens if he trips and falls? This is where the phrase "putting all of your eggs in one basket" comes from. A better solution would be to have 30 five year olds each holding a single egg in both hands while skipping down the road. One or more of them might trip and fall, destroying the egg, but odds are that most of them won't. The 5-year-olds in this example are analogous to CEOs of the companies you are investing in. They are not really careful with your nest egg because it is not their money, but most of them will make it to the market. Strangely, the CEO gets paid whether they destroy your nest egg or not, so it is not wise to give anyone all of your eggs. They get more money if they don't break the egg, but they typically have a golden parachute even if they drive the business into the ground. The concept I have described here is diversification.

One way to do this would be to open a brokerage account and buy 30 different stocks that cover the spread of all public companies available. It turns out that this is difficult to do and very expensive if you don't have at least $300,000 to invest. A better solution for the small investor is called a stock mutual fund. A mutual fund is created by a company that collects investments from many investors, pools their funds and creates a "mutual fund" for each investor to own a part of. They don't do this for free, and typically charge from 0.2 percent up to 3 percent of your assets for this service. I'll speak more about fees later on, but in many cases, it is a good idea to invest using mutual funds. You can buy mutual funds that invest in just about everything under the sun and in virtually every country of the world. I've already described one type of sector specific fund called a REIT that invests only in real estate investment companies. I'll have more to say on which types of funds to invest in later. For now just remember that you need to keep your eggs in more than one basket.

This is especially true if you are a business owner. You should not bet that all your eggs will get to market, even if you are the 5-year-old skipping down the road. I'm sure that you have great confidence in yourself, and may have delivered many eggs to market in the past, but you should not have more than 1/3 of your money invested in any one company, even if that company is your own. Be sure and diversify your money so that any one failure will not wipe you out.

Rule #2) Minimize your expenses.

You should minimize your expenses when you buy stocks, whether it be in a mutual fund or with single stocks. Stock returns tend to be pretty random. One of the few guaranteed ways that have been proven by academics to increase your returns is to minimize your expenses. Financial people have invented a myriad of ways to extract money from your pocket and most of them make a very good living doing so. They play on your fears of living out your retirement years eating cat food and then bleed you dry when they take your money to invest. I do not mean to say that all investment professionals are out to get you. There are some good advisors out there who are trying to help, but none of them work for free. I will note a few of the most common fees and expenses here, but by no means is the following an exhaustive list of the ways people can pilfer your money.

The Mutual Fund Load

My pet peeve with the mutual fund industry is the mutual fund load. The vast majority of mutual fund sales people get paid on commission. This sales commission ranges from 5 to 8 percent and is typically 5 ¾ percent of the money you invest. In other words, the person who sells you a mutual fund takes 5 to 8 percent of the money you give them and pockets it before it ever gets invested in anything! On average, and considering inflation, you have to have your money invested for a year before you make up for supporting the salesman's lifestyle! This type of load is called a front end load. There are also back end loads that are taken off of your investment if you pull the money out of the investment before a given period of time. The salesperson still gets paid up front, but investments with back end loads have higher expense ratios to pay their sales force. When the stock market crashed in 2001/2002, I made the mistake of pulling my money out of the stock market and putting it into a back end loaded bond fund. The sales woman neglected to mention that it was back end loaded, and I got a nasty surprise when I pulled the money out in 2003 to reinvest it in the market.

The good news is that you can buy no-load funds on your own, without the assistance of a sales person. I'll provide more on this later. One argument I hear from these sales people is that loaded funds perform just as well as no-load funds. This is true, when you don't consider the loss of 5–8 percent of your money. The fact of the matter is that many funds are sold both with and without loads! If no-load funds perform as well as loaded funds, why pay the fee? One plausible answer is that the investor simply does not have the financial education to do it himself. I submit that it is better to get educated and understand your investment before you invest. This is the main reason I have written this book. Another answer is that a good investment advisor will help you stay calm and not pull all of your money out of the market when it drops. The market will drop. The only question is when. It may be good to have an advisor help you to stay the course when market corrections or crashes occur.

The Mutual Fund Expense Ratio

The mutual fund expense ratio is the percentage a mutual fund company charges for the service of diversifying your investment and/or selecting stocks. In my opinion, the mutual fund expense ratio is the only valid expense that mutual fund companies charge. However, these fees vary a lot, as I have mentioned from 0.2 percent of your assets to 3 percent of your assets per year. Remember that this is not 3 percent of your gains, but 3 percent of your total assets. If the fund is siphoning off 3 percent and the average return is 7 percent then they have taken 43 percent of your return! When the stock market drops they still take a percentage of your assets, exacerbating the loss to your nest egg. This is not a good plan! Once again, they are guaranteed to make their money while you take all the risk, though they make more money if you make money. Active mutual fund managers claim that their superior stock picking capabilities more than make up for their fees. Academicians have found that this is not true. In fact, the stock pickers do just a little better than monkeys picking random stocks. When you consider their fees they do even worse (monkeys work for food while stock pickers are some of the highest paid professionals). There are, of course, some mutual fund managers who do better than the market. This is mainly due to luck. There have been a handful of managers that have statistically done better than could be accounted for by luck, but it is even harder to find these guys than it is to pick stocks that will go up. One reason for this is that when a manager does well, he ends up with piles of money to invest and it is harder to get great returns with piles of money than it is with small amounts of money. This is because any move he makes with piles of money tends to move the market prices before he completes the move. You have to find the great money manager before they are well known as a great manager. For more information on this topic read *A Random Walk Down Wall Street*, by Burton G. Malkiel.

So what is an investor to do?

The answer is passively managed mutual funds. A passive manager does not try to beat market returns, but simply tries to buy all of the market, or emulate a specific index. There are many indexes that are emulated by passively managed mutual funds. The first index fund, as these are called, was the S&P 500 index fund created by Jack Bogle, the CEO of the Vanguard Mutual Fund Company. He theorized that mutual fund pickers were much like monkeys in suits getting paid a lot of money to provide little value. His plan was to minimize expenses and give investors the opportunity to invest in the stock market at cost. He was laughed to scorn when he took over Vanguard decades ago, but has been instrumental in making the Vanguard

Company the largest mutual fund company to date. It turns out that passively managed mutual fund companies charge less than 0.5 percent to provide the service of diversification, and often charge less than 0.2 percent of assets for this service. As a result, these funds on average beat 2/3 of mutual funds on the market. Most mutual fund companies now offer index funds that the average investor can take advantage of, but Vanguard is the only non-profit mutual fund company out there, which is why I recommend their products. To provide complete disclosure I do have some of my money invested with Vanguard, but I do not get any fees, commissions or kickbacks of any kind for recommending their services. I only get good returns on my investments.

12b1 Mutual Fund Marketing Fees

Some fund companies have the audacity to charge what is called a 12b1 fee on top of the expense ratio. These fees were designed to hide the mutual fund load. They use the excuse that they need to market their products and ask you to pay for the marketing expenses. They want you to pay for them to market the fund to other unsuspecting customers. You should not walk, but run from a salesman peddling a fund with 12b1 fees in addition to the expense ratio. The fact of the matter is that the first stock mutual fund I purchased was a loaded fund with 12b1 fees. When I first graduated college, I was sold the fund with the unguaranteed promise that it would go up 10 percent per year. I then went to work for a company that used Vanguard for their 401k and I noticed that my Vanguard 401k investments did significantly better than my loaded, super high fee fund. I promptly opened an IRA with Vanguard and moved my funds over and have never regretted the move.

Rule #3) Buy low and sell high.

It is a fact that if you could manage to buy when the market is at its lowest and sell when it is at its highest you could make a killing. If you could figure out how to do this, you would do much better than investing for the long term in an index fund. The problem is that doing so is next to impossible. Even if you could figure out how to buy when the market is at its bottom, or even near its bottom, you still have to know when to sell. It is very difficult to know when to sell. Even traditional fundamental investors struggle with this. A fundamental investor is a person who tries to figure out the actual value of a company, based on the assets a company holds, its ability to innovate, its profit margin, etc. Consider 1996 when the Federal Reserve Chairman Alan Greenspan made his famous statement about the markets using the phrase "Irrational Exuberance." The irrational exuberance went on for another 5 years and had you sold in 1996, you would've lost a fortune. However, if you are like most people, you didn't sell in 2001, so you lost a fortune anyway. My point is that it is very difficult to time the markets, and perhaps even more difficult than it is to pick the right stocks.

So how does one buy low and sell high? The answer is portfolio allocation. Portfolio allocation is the only way that I know to buy low and sell high on a regular basis. The concept is pretty simple. You pick a percentage of stocks and bonds that you want to own and you stick with it year in and year out. If stocks go up, then you sell some stocks at the end of the year and buy bonds. If stocks go down and/or bonds go up faster than stocks, then you sell some bonds at the end of the year and buy stocks. This way you are guaranteed to sell high and buy low. The key is to have the discipline to stick to your strategy. It sounds easier than it really is. It is a simple concept that is hard to execute because we are all emotional beings. When stocks are flying high, it is REALLY hard to sell them and buy bonds. Similarly, when stocks have tanked and the financial pundits are reporting that the world has come to an end, it is equally difficult to sell your bonds and buy stocks. However, if you can pull this off, you will be rewarded with about a one percent premium on your portfolio returns. One percent may not seem like much, but over the years, it can be HUGE. Go back to Chapter 5 on the time value of money and look at the difference between a 6 percent and 7 percent return on $503 dollars per month invested over 40 years. The answer is about $300,000. If you save a percent by buying low cost mutual funds and a percent by utilizing portfolio allocation, you will be greatly ahead on your path to becoming wealthy!

Step 6) Diversify your investments with debt and real estate assets as you get older.

As John Bon Jovi says, "I'm not old, I'm just older." The reality of investing is that it takes time, and as time goes by we get older and cannot afford to take as much risk as when we are young. The stock market has gone for periods as long as 20 years with no real returns. After the crash of 1929, the market had practically a zero percent return for 20 years as people hid their money in their mattresses or in jars in the ground. I do not think this will happen again, but we recently viewed ten years of similarly dismal returns. If you are 60 years old and 100 percent invested in stocks, you are tempting the fates to require you to work for the rest of your life. If you decide to quit your job when the market is down and you have most of your money in stocks, you could significantly reduce the quality of your lifestyle during your golden years.

So what percentage of stocks should you own? I recommend subtracting your age from 100 and holding that percentage of stocks in your portfolio. I recommend doing this because it ensures that you will have at least some money in stocks for the vast majority of your life span. It also ensures that you will have some money in other investments that you can use for portfolio allocation, described earlier. The truth is that over long periods of time (20 years or more), you would be better off having all of your money in stocks. However, you don't always have 20 years, and if you die or need your money while the market is down, then you will regret holding it all in stocks. The older you get, the more likely it is that you will not be able to work and keep investing. See the chart below. I will call the "other investments" fixed income investments. These are bonds, certificates of deposit, money market accounts, real estate, commodities, such as gold and art, etc. The fixed income investments are anything with a market value that you are saving for the time when you quit your day job.

	Investments	
Age	percent Stock	percent Fixed Income
5	95	5
10	90	10
15	85	15
20	80	20
25	75	25
30	70	30
35	65	35
40	60	40
45	55	45
50	50	50
55	45	55
60	40	60
65	35	65
70	30	70
75	25	75
80	20	80
85	15	85
90	10	90
95	5	95
100	0	100

Every year, on your birthday or some other date that is easy for you to remember, tally up how much stock you have and rebalance your percentage of stock to be equal to 100 minus your age. This is extremely simple and a time tested way to become wealthy without taking on too much risk. Remember how I wrote that the most simple investment plan is the best? Here you have it. Spend your time with your loved ones, earning a living and serving others. Don't spend all of your time fiddling with your investment portfolio. Messing with your investments is proven to LOWER your returns. I know this is counter-intuitive, but it is true.

Some people will argue that this investment advice is too conservative. Others will argue that it is too risky. Don't believe them! Test it out for yourselves. Try it for 10 years and see if the advice rings true. I have, for the last 10 years and it has served me well over two major recessions. I bought stocks when the market was low and sold them when it was high and made money. You can too. If you really can't stand being this risky or this conservative, then subtract or add 20 percent to the percentage of stocks you own. See the table below. The most important thing to remember is that you need to make a plan and stick to it! Don't use the aggressive plan when the stock market is booming and switch to conservative when it tanks again. It's more important to be consistent than it is to be aggressive or conservative!

	Aggressive Investments			Conservative Investments	
	Percent	Percent Fixed		Percent	Percent Fixed
Age	Stock	Income	Age	Stock	Income
5	100	0	5	75	25
10	100	0	10	70	30
15	100	0	15	65	35
20	100	0	20	60	40
25	95	5	25	55	45
30	90	10	30	50	50
35	85	15	35	45	55
40	80	20	40	40	60
45	75	25	45	35	65
50	70	30	50	30	70
55	65	35	55	25	75
60	60	40	60	20	80
65	55	45	65	15	85
70	50	50	70	10	90
75	45	55	75	5	95
80	40	60	80	0	100
85	35	65	85	0	100
90	30	70	90	0	100
95	25	75	95	0	100
100	20	80	100	0	100

Looking at your investments once a year is about the right frequency for viewing your fund performance if you are invested in stock market mutual funds that cover the entire market. Never look at your investments more often than quarterly. The reason is that we are emotional creatures. If the market is tanking and you are watching the value of your portfolio drop on a daily basis you will be highly tempted to yank all of your money out of stocks, buy a CD (or bond fund as I did) and sit in the corner rocking while you suck your thumb. Similarly, if the market is shooting up, you will be tempted to mortgage your house to buy internet stocks or you will miss out on the boom. I knew a guy who had five high end BMWs that he had acquired in the late 90s when the market was gangbusters. I'm not sure why he needed five, but he lost them all and his big house when the market tanked. He now drives a Mini-Cooper, still a nice car, but nothing like what he was driving before. He has a picture on his office wall of him sitting in front of his 5 bimmers parked in front of the house he lost to remind him not to make the same mistake again. Don't risk it all or hide in fixed income investments and do worse than inflation. Make a plan and stick to it and you will be better off than 90 percent of the population!

What should the "fixed income" portion of your portfolio be? I recommend putting half in debt investments and half in hard assets. I define a debt investment as money that you loan other people in return for a return of your principal, plus interest. Examples of these are Bonds, CDs, Money Market Mutual Funds, savings accounts, etc. Hard assets are things that you buy that are tangible items you can see, feel and touch. Examples of these are real estate, precious metals and gems, collectibles, etc. Do not include your emergency fund, or your cars in this analysis. Anything that you need on a daily basis should not be included in this analysis, including your primary residence. Include only things that you could sell to support yourself. If you follow my plan you will have 1/3 in stock, 1/3 in debt assets and 1/3 in hard assets when you are the typical retirement age. You will be ready for whatever comes your way. Picture yourself sitting on a three-legged stool, called your retirement seat, when you are ready to quit your job. The three legs are stocks, hard assets (real estate) and debt assets (bonds).

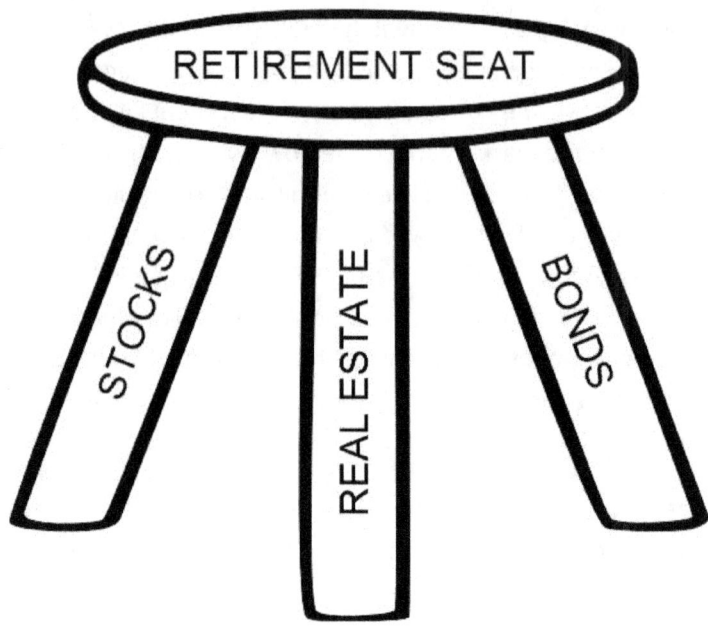

So how is all of this to be done? What investments should you invest in? Another of my pet peeves is reading an investment book that does not tell the reader what to invest in. I will provide two examples here that show you how to implement exactly what I described above. These examples run the gamut from brain dead to easy. As I said before, I don't recommend any investment plan that is hard to follow or difficult to understand. Never invest in anything you don't understand! Also keep in mind that I don't take any responsibility for the performance of your investments. Stock investments are risky, and even more risky for novice investors. I will use Vanguard funds as examples of what I recommend, but similar funds are available from many other discount brokerage companies, including Fidelity, T. Rowe Price, Schwab, etc.

The Brain Dead Investment Portfolio

A new breed of funds has emerged of late called Target Date Retirement Funds. These are basically funds of funds that are automatically rebalanced by the fund manager. In other words, these are funds that contain a number of other funds. For the person new to investing in the stock market, these are what I recommend. A fund manager picks two or more bond or stock funds and rebalances them every year as you get older. You pick one with a target date nearest the date when you want to quit your day job. You then set up an automatic transfer of your investment money every month to the account and forget about it. You will likely have an option like this in your 401k. Complain to the human resources department of your company if a target date retirement fund is not available. If you don't have a 401k, or your 401k doesn't have a target date retirement fund, then set up an IRA and set up your automatic investment to go out once a month. Once you have the automatic investment set up, you can forget about these accounts until you are ready to retire. Go to the following URL and click on the link that corresponds to your age. Read about the fund and make sure you fully understand it before you invest. If you don't understand, you may want to call Vanguard (or the broker of your choice) and ask questions. They are typically more than happy to answer any questions that you ask in order to get your money.

https://personal.vanguard.com/us/funds/vanguard/TargetRetirementList

The trick to the target date retirement fund is that they are not all created equal. Some funds favor a higher percentage of stocks than others. Be sure to investigate the fund holdings and risk profile before investing. You can pick more aggressive or less aggressive funds by tweaking the target date or switching investment companies. The other caveat to investing in this manner is that the expense ratios are typically higher. The reason they are higher is you have to pay the fund manager to do the portfolio allocation for you. You pay an expense for the target date fund, and you also pay an expense for the funds he invests in. If you want to lower your expenses, do the rebalancing yourself as I describe below.

The Easy Investment Portfolio

The Easy Investment Portfolio consists of two mutual funds. One fund is composed of stocks and the other of bonds. Use the tables listed above to rebalance the two funds once a year on your birthday (just to help you remember to rebalance). I recommend investing in funds that cover the entire world, with percentages based on the size of the stock markets throughout the world. Currently, U.S. stocks make up about 40 percent of the market valuations of stocks throughout the world, so I recommend investing in a fund that follows this percentage. Look for an index fund that follows the FTSE International Index. The stock fund I recommend for this is the Vanguard Total World Stock Index Fund Investor Shares (VTWSX). The expense ratios for this type of fund run a little higher than domestic funds because it is more expensive and difficult to invest internationally. Don't pay more than a 1 percent expense ratio for an index fund like this. Despite this expense, I still think they are worth looking into because the diversification that is offered by funds like this is incredible.

The bond fund that I recommend investing in is Vanguard's Total Bond Market index (VBMFX). This fund invests 30 percent of its money in corporate bonds, which are a bit riskier, and the rest in U.S. government bonds that are nearly the most stable investment that one can make. I do not think that international exposure is required in a bond fund simply because you are loaning your money to an entity, and that can be done anywhere in the world. The idea of having a bond fund is to have a low risk pile of money that you can use to buy stocks with when they are down and to put your money into when you sell stocks that are up. I don't believe that you need to go overseas to get this kind of investment.

There have been studies that show there is some advantage to breaking out the stock portion of your portfolio into additional pieces. For example, you could break your stocks into small and large cap stocks or break them into domestic (U.S. stock) and international (everywhere else). The idea is that sometimes large cap stocks do better than small caps and vice versa. Similarly, sometimes U.S. stocks do better than international stocks and vice versa. If you have each of these in different mutual funds, you can rebalance them yearly or even semi-annually and get a fraction of a percentage point improvement. It is OK to do this kind of diversification, but don't go crazy doing so. The idea is to keep investing simple because the most simple investment strategies are the ones you are most likely to stick to. Don't play around with more than 5 mutual funds, unless you want to make a hobby of investing. It is more lucrative to take a second job or start a part time business than it is to be constantly tweaking your portfolio.

Bonds are one of the simplest ways to diversify. You loan your money to an entity such as a company or government, and they agree to return your money to you at a later date, plus interest. Note that the value of bonds will fluctuate before the bond matures with interest rates, but if you hold the bond to maturity you will get exactly what the bond contract dictates unless the entity goes bankrupt. Bond funds are like mutual funds in that a group of people invest their money together in order to reduce the risk that any one entity will go bankrupt. The bond fund manager then has to decide which bonds to buy and when to sell. Again, I recommend going with a passive bond fund manager to reduce expense ratios. If the bond fund is only yielding 4 percent and the management company takes 1 percent, then you are blowing 25 percent of your money on a task that is relatively simple to do. Peter Lynch compares this to paying Yo Yo Ma to play the radio (instead of the cello). This is a very simplistic explanation of bonds. Some folks spend their whole lives and careers studying and investing in bonds.

I want to mention a note about risk here. Bonds funds are subject to interest rate risk. As interest rates go up, the value of a bond fund will go down. The reason for this is that if you borrow money at 3 percent from an entity and interest rates go up to 5 percent, then your "loan" to the entity will be worth less than new loans at 5 percent. The longer the term for the bond fund, the higher the interest rate risk. 30 year bonds are much more susceptible to this type of risk than one year treasury notes. At the writing of this book, the interest rates in the U.S. are at record lows and have only one direction to go; up. As a result, the interest rate risk is high. One might consider using a one year certificate of deposit (CD) for the fixed income part of his portfolio now instead of a bond fund due to interest rate risk. The downside to this plan is that CDs typically offer lower interest rates than bonds do. Right now VBMFX is yielding about 2 ½ percent while 1 year CDs are yielding about 1 percent. It is up to you whether or not you want to take the extra risk to get the additional one and a half percent return.

Certificates of Deposit (CDs) are another way to diversify your investments. The value of CDs do not fluctuate over time, but CDs typically have penalties associated with pulling your money out before they mature. They also typically pay a lower interest rate than do bonds or other investments. Banks like to offer CDs because they can pay you a low rate of interest and invest that money in higher paying loans or investments. For example, they borrow money from you at 1 percent and then loan it to someone else at 4 percent for a mortgage or even 8 percent for a credit card. CDs are usually insured by the government against default by the bank, so the risk of these investments is lower than for bonds. I personally don't like CDs because of their low rate of return.

Another so called fixed income investment is the money market fund. This is like a bond fund, only that the fund managers typically invest in very conservative investments, like short term government notes. The managers have the goal of keeping the value of the fund as close to $1 as possible so that its share does not fluctuate much more than a savings account. These types of accounts are great for emergency funds and short term savings.

Once you have built up a decent amount of savings (think six figures), you can diversify your holdings into other types of assets than stocks and bonds. Real estate is my favorite way to diversify your investments. I already discussed buying your personal residence and investing in REITs. If you love real estate, you should consider buying an investment property. If you do so, make sure to put at least 25 percent down and increase your emergency fund to include a 6 month supply of ALL your expenses, including those associated with the rental property. As always, paying cash is less risky than going into debt to buy assets. One of the benefits of real estate is that you have tenants to pay the maintenance, taxes and mortgage if you hold a loan on the property. Another benefit is that the government allows you to depreciate the property. This means that you can write off a portion of the amount you paid for the improvements on the property every year you own it until the value goes to zero over a 27 1/2 year period. The idea is that the government thinks any improvements to a property go away over about a 27 ½ year period. The reality is that many properties go UP in value over time and not down. The problem with this plan is that your cost basis also goes down as you depreciate it over the years. When you sell the property, you will have to pay capital gains taxes based on your cost basis.

Your cost basis is the amount that you paid for a property. When you sell an investment property, you will owe capital gains taxes on the difference between the selling price and your cost basis. When you depreciate the property, the cost basis goes down and you owe more tax when you sell. As of the writing of this book, investors are also allowed to write off the interest paid on the mortgage even when the renter is paying it! If you decide to buy real estate as an investment, I recommend getting a certified public accountant to help with the tax issues, which can get complicated. I have not mentioned the difficulty of managing tenants in rental property. This can be relatively easy or a complete nightmare, and how to do so properly is beyond the scope of this book. For a fee, rental property management companies will do this for you. To avoid the complications of owning your own real estate, you could invest in REITs as previously mentioned. Just keep in mind that the more involved you are, or the more work that is required, the higher the potential return on investment. Rental properties that are properly managed can earn more than stocks, but typically require more work. There are two advantages that investing in real estate has over investing in stocks: 1) The value of real estate typically will not go to zero like a stock does when the company goes out of business. Even if the house is completely trashed and needs to be torn down, the land underneath should retain some value. 2) No one is making any more land to build property on, but the population is increasing every year. The latter advantage is not as great as it might seem. If you have ever flown over Texas or the middle part of America, you should note that there is plenty of space for expansion. If, however, you buy property near a metropolitan area, the value of the property will likely go up over time to the tune of 1 percent to 2 percent above inflation. Not as good as stocks, but less risky when you hold home owners insurance on the property. Similar to stocks, the value of real estate goes up and down as it did toward the end of the first decade of the 21st

century. Don't let the real estate broker tell you that real estate always goes up and never goes down.

Other hard assets to invest in as you get older are precious metals, gems and collectibles. I don't recommend investing in these types of assets unless you have a great deal of knowledge about them. These can be some of the most risky investments of all AND they don't provide dividend, interest or rental income to offset that risk. They are speculative at best and outright gambling at worst. Even if you have a lot of knowledge about a certain type commodity or collectable, I don't recommend investing more that 10 percent of your portfolio in this type of asset. However, if you have a hobby like gun collecting or a love for art, you may get non-financial benefits from investing in this area.

As I have mentioned before, the best investment strategy is the simplest. Stocks, bonds and real estate are a simple way to invest and will provide you with a great retirement seat to sit on through your waning years.

Step 7) Quit your day job, if you want to.

Quit your day job, once the income from your investments is double your expenses. Step 7 is the goal that you have been striving for most of your life. If you have reached this point, congratulations! You have earned the right to do what you want to do and are not beholden to employers, customers or anyone else. It is also the time where you can focus on leaving your mark on the world. Do you want to leave a legacy to your kids or grandkids? Do you want to donate your money or your time to charity? Do you want to retire to a warm climate and play games for the rest of your life? Do you want to travel the world and see what it has to offer? The options are numerous, and this is the time to fully pursue your dreams.

Why do I say double your expenses? The fact of the matter is that expenses vary a lot. When you reach Step 7, you may be in perfect health but later have to deal with increased medical expenses. The return on your investments may also vary over time, so you need to be prepared. Also, if you follow the instructions in this book, you should be either out of debt or close to out of debt by this point. If you have kids, they have likely moved out and living on their own; at least one can hope! Your expenses should be relatively low, making them easier to double with your investments. It is also simply fun to continue to have a positive cash flow to spend, invest, or give away at this time in your life.

There is no specific age at which you need to reach for Step 7. If you get to this point before the age the government thinks you should "retire", congratulations. Step 7 is not retirement, but changing your life such that you do only the work you want to do. If you have found a job that you love, as I suggest in Chapter 4, "Live Within Your Means," you may want to keep working at your job full time or part time. Quitting your day job, if you want to, is the reward for making the sacrifices necessary to become wealthy. I don't recommend that you ever stop contributing to society unless your health prevents you from doing so. If you don't want to work for an income once you reach step 7, then find a place to donate your time. You may find more enjoyment and personal rewards from doing so than you ever did by working for money. Then again, you may love your job and find great satisfaction in building a business or mentoring others.

The point is that in step 7 you are free to do what you want. I hope this book will help you reach your dreams by becoming financially free. I also hope that you enjoyed reading it as much as I enjoyed writing it. Good luck and may you become as WEALTHI as you want to be, for it is truly up to you.

Appendix A: Recommended Reading

Don't let your financial education end with this book. Here is some additional readying that I recommend.

1. A Random Walk Down Wall Street: The Time-Tested Strategy for Successful Investing, by Burton G. Malkiel
2. On Fire: The 7 Choices to Ignite a Radically Inspired Life, by John O'Leary
3. Rich Dad, Poor Dad: What The Rich Teach their Kids About Money That the Poor and Middle Class Do Not! by Robert T. Kiyosaki
4. The 7 Habits of Highly Effective People, by Stephen R. Covey
5. The Automatic Millionaire: A Powerful One-Step Plan to Live and Finish Rich, by David Bach
6. The Millionaire Mind, by William J. Stanley
7. The Millionaire Next Door: The Surprising Secrets of America's Wealthy, by William J. Stanley and Thomas D. Denko
8. The Total Money Makeover: A Proven Plan for Financial Fitness, by Dave Ramsey

Appendix B: Calculating Compound Interest

There are 5 basic variables and corresponding equations that will allow you to calculate 90 percent of the data you need to help you become wealthy. They are Future Value (FV), Present Value (PV), Payment (PMT), interest rate (RATE) and term (NPER) calculations. NPER is an abbreviation for the number of periods in the calculation. Sometimes the interest rate is designated with the percent sign (%). There are a few tricky things to remember when doing financial calculations. The first is that the interest rate always corresponds to the time period. If you are using a year as a time period then you must enter the yearly rate and if you are using a month (as with a mortgage payment calculation) then you must use the monthly rate, which is simply the yearly rate divided by 12. Make sure you know which time period is set on your calculator. Check the user's manual to set the time period. The other tricky part is to know whether in the interest rate is calculated at the beginning or end of the time period. The default is typically at the end of the time period, but you need to make sure it is set that way.

How to use a financial calculator to calculate compound interest

On a financial calculator there are 5 buttons across the top of the calculator that correspond to the quantities described above. If you have 4 of the values you can get the 5th by entering them into a financial calculator. Let's start with the future value calculations that I used to create the tables shown in chapter 5. For a future value calculation you don't have the future value, but you do have the estimated interest rate, the term, the payment and the present value. For the present value I have used $0.00 as most people just starting out on their financial education are broke with no significant retirement savings. If you have some then you can enter them into the calculator.

1) Type in your current retirement savings into the calculator and hit the PV button. Be sure and put a negative sign in front of the value. The way I like to think of the negative sign is when money is coming out of your pocket the sign is negative. When it is coming into your pocket it is positive. You have to take some money out of your pocket in order to invest it in hopes of getting a return on your investment. In this example we will use 0 as the present value.

2) Type in the amount of time you have left before retirement in months. For example, if you have 25 years to retirement then type in 25 X 12 or 300 and hit the NPER button.

3) Note that interest rates are typically entered into a calculator in decimal format and not as percentages. A six percent interest rate is equal to .06 on the calculator. Type the yearly interest rate you expect to achieve into the calculator and divide it by 12 as you will be entering monthly payments and hit the RATE button. For this example let's assume a 6 percent annual return or .06 / 12 = .005.

4) The last thing to enter is your monthly investment. Type this into the calculator with a negative sign in front of the number and hit the pmt button. For example, if you plan to save $500/month then type in -500 and hit the PMT button.

5) To solve the calculation then don't type anything else in and hit the FV button and the solution will be displayed on the screen.

Assuming that you started with a present value of 0, the solution to this simple problem is $346,496.98.

Let's do one more example. Let's say you want to buy a house with a 15 year loan. Suppose that you are buying an average house that costs $215,000 and you are putting 20 percent down and paying the closing costs, so the principal on the loan is $172,000. This is the present value for the problem. The annual interest rate is 6 percent and the term is 15 years or 180 months. What would you suppose the payment would be on such a loan? You don't have to guess anymore.

1) Type in 172000 and press the present value button (PV).
2) Type in .005 and hit the rate (%) button.
3) Type in 180 and hit the term (NPER) button.
4) Type in 0 and hit the future value button (FV).
5) Hit the payment (PMT) button and the answer will be displayed on the screen.

The answer to this problem is $1,451.43. Once you have the hang of it, figure out the monthly payment for your own house if you were to switch to a 15 year loan or if you don't own a house then determine how much the monthly principal and interest on a house would cost if you were to buy.

If you want to do the calculations in Microsoft Excel or Works Spreadsheet then the formulas are also simple. For example, to calculate a future value, type the following into a cell, =fv(rate, nper, pv, pmt, type), where the 'rate' is the interest rate, the 'nper' is the number of payments, the 'pv' is the present value, the 'pmt' is the payment and the 'type' variable tells the spreadsheet whether you want the interest calculated at the beginning or end of the time period. The default is at the end, so you can leave that field blank. The same goes for the present value if the present value is 0. See the table below for a full list of Microsoft Spreadsheet equations.

Appendix B: Calculating Compound Interest

Future Value (FV)	=fv(rate, nper, pv, pmt, type)
Payment (PMT)	=pmt(rate, nper, pv, fv, type)
Present Value (PV)	=pv(rate, nper, pmt, fv, type)
Term (NPER)	=nper(rate, pmt, pv, fv, type)
Interest Rate (RATE)	=rate(nper, pmt, pv, fv, type)

I find it convenient to put each of the known variables into their own cell and then reference each cell in the equation. That way you can vary the known variables to run different scenarios without having to retype the equations. Let's do the same examples shown above in Excel.

The equation entered in cell B2 is "=FV(B2,B3,B4,B5)"

A COLUMN	B COLUMN
Future Value	$346,496.98
Interest Rate	0.005
Term (nper)	300
Payment	-500
Present Value	0

Now let's do the second problem in Excel. The equation entered in cell B2 is "=PMT(B2,B3,B4,B5)"

A COLUMN	B COLUMN
Payment	($1,451.43)
Interest Rate	0.005
Term (nper)	180
Future Value	0
Present Value	172000

The parenthesis in Excel (and generally in accounting) means the number is a negative value.